The Rival Ladies by John Dryden

A Tragi-Comedy

John Dryden was born on August 9th, 1631 in the village rectory of Aldwincle near Thrapston in Northamptonshire. As a boy Dryden lived in the nearby village of Titchmarsh, Northamptonshire. In 1644 he was sent to Westminster School as a King's Scholar.

Dryden obtained his BA in 1654, graduating top of the list for Trinity College, Cambridge that year.

Returning to London during The Protectorate, Dryden now obtained work with Cromwell's Secretary of State, John Thurloe.

At Cromwell's funeral on 23 November 1658 Dryden was in the company of the Puritan poets John Milton and Andrew Marvell. The setting was to be a sea change in English history. From Republic to Monarchy and from one set of lauded poets to what would soon become the Age of Dryden.

The start began later that year when Dryden published the first of his great poems, Heroic Stanzas (1658), a eulogy on Cromwell's death.

With the Restoration of the Monarchy in 1660 Dryden celebrated in verse with Astraea Redux, an authentic royalist panegyric.

With the re opening of the theatres after the Puritan ban, Dryden began to also write plays. His first play, The Wild Gallant, appeared in 1663 but was not successful. From 1668 on he was contracted to produce three plays a year for the King's Company, in which he became a shareholder. During the 1660s and '70s, theatrical writing was his main source of income.

In 1667, he published Annus Mirabilis, a lengthy historical poem which described the English defeat of the Dutch naval fleet and the Great Fire of London in 1666. It established him as the pre-eminent poet of his generation, and was crucial in his attaining the posts of Poet Laureate (1668) and then historiographer royal (1670).

This was truly the Age of Dryden, he was the foremost English Literary figure in Poetry, Plays, translations and other forms.

In 1694 he began work on what would be his most ambitious and defining work as translator, The Works of Virgil (1697), which was published by subscription. It was a national event.

John Dryden died on May 12th, 1700, and was initially buried in St. Anne's cemetery in Soho, before being exhumed and reburied in Westminster Abbey ten days later.

Index of Contents

PROLOGUE

This play, like that which preceded it, is a drama of intrigue, borrowed from the Spanish, and claiming merit only in proportion to the diversity and ingenuity of the incidents represented. On this point every reader can decide for himself; and it would be an invidious task to point out blemishes, where, to own the truth, there are but few beauties. The ease with which the affections of almost every female in the drama are engrossed by Gonsalvo, and afterwards transferred to the lovers, upon whom the winding up of the plot made it necessary to devolve them, will, it is probable, strike every reader as unnatural. In truth, when the depraved appetite of the public requires to be gratified by trick and bustle, instead of nature and sentiment, authors must sacrifice the probable, as well as the simple, process of events.

The author seems principally to have valued himself on this piece, because it contains some scenes executed in rhyme, in what was then called the heroic manner. Upon this opinion, which Dryden lived to retract, I have ventured to offer my sentiments in the Life of the Author. In other respects, though not slow in perceiving and avouching his own merit, our author seems to consider the Rival Ladies as no very successful dramatic effort.

The Rival Ladies is supposed to have been first acted in 1663, and was certainly published in the year following. Of its success we know nothing particular. It is probable, the flowing verse, into which some part of the dialogue is thrown, with the strong point and antithesis, which distinguishes Dryden's works, and particularly his argumentative poetry, tended to redeem the credit of the author of the Wild Gallant.

THE RIGHT HONOURABLE ROGER, EARL OF ORRERY[1].

[Footnote 1: This distinguished person was fifth son of Richard Boyle, known by the title of the great Earl of Cork. His first title was Lord Broghill, under which he distinguished himself in Ireland. Cromwell, although his lordship was a noted royalist, and in actual correspondence with the exiled monarch, had so much confidence in his honour and talents, that he almost compelled him to act as lord lieutenant of that kingdom, under the stipulation that he was to come under no oaths, and only to act against the rebel Irish, then the common enemy. He was instrumental in the restoration, and *created earl of Orrery by Charles II, in 1660, He deserved Dryden's panegyric in every respect, except as a poet—the very character, however, in which he is most complimented, and perhaps was best pleased to be so. He wrote, 1st, The Art of War—2d, Parthenissa, a romance—3d, Some Poems—4th; Eight Plays—5th, State Tracts.]*

My Lord,

This worthless present was designed you long before it was a play; when it was only a confused mass of thoughts, tumbling over one another in the dark; when the fancy was yet in its first work, moving the sleeping images of things towards the light, there to be distinguished, and then either chosen or rejected by the judgment; it was yours, my lord, before I could call it mine. And, I confess, in that first tumult of my thoughts, there appeared a disorderly kind of beauty in some of them, which gave me hope, something, worthy my lord of Orrery, might be drawn from them: But I was then in that eagerness of imagination, which, by overpleasing fanciful men, flatters them into the danger of writing; so that, when I had moulded it into that shape it now bears, I looked with such disgust upon it, that the censures of our severest critics are charitable to what I thought (and still think) of it myself: It is so far from me to believe this perfect, that I am apt to conclude our best plays are scarcely so; for the stage being the representation of the world, and the actions in it, how can it be imagined, that the picture of human life can be more exact than life itself is? He may be allowed sometimes to err, who undertakes to move so many characters and humours, as are requisite in a play, in those narrow channels which are proper to each of them; to conduct his imaginary persons through so many various intrigues and chances, as the labouring audience shall think them lost under every billow; and then, at length, to work them so naturally out of their distresses, that, when the whole plot is laid open, the spectators may rest satisfied, that every cause was powerful enough to produce the effect it had; and that the whole chain of them was with such due order linked together, that the first accident would naturally beget the second, till they all rendered the conclusion necessary.

These difficulties, my lord, may reasonably excuse the errors of my undertaking; but for this confidence of my dedication, I have an argument, which is too advantageous for me not to publish it to the world. It is the kindness your lordship has continually shown to all my writings. You have been pleased, my lord, they should sometimes cross the Irish seas, to kiss your hands; which passage (contrary to the experience of others) I have found the least dangerous in the world. Your favour has shone upon me at a remote distance, without the least knowledge of my person; and (like the influence of the heavenly bodies) you have done good, without knowing to whom you did it. It is this virtue in your lordship, which emboldens me to this attempt; for, did I not consider you as my patron, I have little reason to desire you for my judge; and should appear with as much awe before you in the reading, as I had when the full theatre sat upon the action. For, who could so severely judge of faults as he, who has given testimony he commits none? Your excellent poems have afforded that knowledge of it to the world, that your enemies are ready to upbraid you with it, as a crime for a man of business to write so well. Neither durst I have justified your lordship in it, if examples of it had not been in the world before you; if Xenophon had not written a romance, and a certain Roman, called Augustus Caesar, a tragedy, and epigrams. But their writing was the entertainment of their pleasure; yours is only a diversion of your pain. The muses have seldom employed your thoughts, but when some violent fit of the gout has snatched you from affairs of state; and, like the priestess of Apollo, you never come to deliver his oracles, but unwillingly, and in torment. So that we are obliged to your lordship's misery for our delight: You treat us with the cruel pleasure of a Turkish triumph, where those, who cut and wound their bodies, sing songs of victory as they pass, and divert others with their own sufferings. Other men endure their diseases; your lordship only can enjoy them. Plotting and writing in this kind are certainly more troublesome employments than many which signify more, and are of greater moment in the world: The fancy, memory, and judgment, are then extended (like so many limbs) upon the rack; all of them reaching with their utmost stress at nature; a thing so almost infinite and boundless, as can never fully be comprehended, but where the images of all things are always present. Yet I wonder not your lordship succeeds so well in this attempt; the knowledge of men is your daily practice in the world; to work and bend their stubborn minds, which go not all after the same grain, but each of them so particular a way, that the same common humours, in several persons, must be wrought upon by several means. Thus, my lord, your sickness is but the imitation of your health; the poet but subordinate to the statesman in you; you still govern men with the same address, and manage business with the same prudence; allowing it here (as in the world) the due increase and growth, till it comes to the just height; and then turning it when it is fully ripe, and nature calls out, as it were, to be delivered. With this only advantage of ease to you in your poetry, that you have fortune here at your command; with which wisdom does often unsuccessfully struggle in the world. Here is no chance, which you have not foreseen; all your heroes are more than your subjects, they are your creatures; and though they seem to move freely in all the sallies of their passions, yet you make destinies for them, which they cannot shun. They are moved (if I may dare to say so) like the rational creatures of the Almighty Poet, who walk at liberty, in their own opinion, because their fetters are invisible; when, indeed, the prison of their will is the more sure for being large; and, instead of an absolute power over their actions, they have only a wretched desire of doing that, which they cannot chuse but do[1].

[Footnote 1: The earl of Orrery was author of several plays. If the reader is not disposed to admit, that his habit of composing them, when tormented by the gout, enhanced their value, it may be allowed to apologise for their faults.]

I have dwelt, my lord, thus long upon your writing, not because you deserve not greater and more noble commendations, but because I am not equally able to express them in other subjects. Like an ill swimmer, I have willingly staid long in my own depth; and though I am eager of performing more, yet am loth to venture out beyond my knowledge: for beyond your poetry, my lord, all is ocean to me. To speak of you as a soldier, or a statesman, were only to betray my own ignorance; and I could hope no better success from it, than that miserable rhetorician had, who solemnly declaimed before Hannibal, of the conduct of armies, and the art of war. I can only say, in general, that the souls of other men shine out at little crannies; they understand some one thing, perhaps, to admiration, while they are darkened on all the other parts; but your lordship's soul is an entire globe of light, breaking out on every side; and, if I have only discovered one beam of it, it is not that the light falls unequally, but because the body, which receives it, is of unequal parts.

The acknowledgment of which is a fair occasion offered me, to retire from the consideration of your lordship to that of myself. I here present you, my lord, with that in print, which you had the goodness not to dislike upon the stage; and account it happy to have met you here in England; it being, at best, like small wines, to be drunk out upon the place, and has not body enough to endure the sea.

I know not whether I have been so careful of the plot and language as I ought; but, for the latter, I have endeavoured to write English, as near as I could distinguish it from the tongue of pedants, and that of affected travellers. Only I am sorry, that (speaking so noble a language as we do) we have not a more certain measure of it, as they have in France, where they have an academy erected for that purpose, and endowed with large privileges by the present king. I wish we might at length leave to borrow words from other nations, which is now a wantonness in us, not a necessity; but so long as some affect to speak them, there will not want others, who will have the boldness to write them.

But I fear, lest, defending the received words, I shall be accused for following the new way, I mean, of writing scenes in verse. Though, to speak properly, it is not so much a new way amongst us, as an old way new revived; for, many years before Shakspeare's plays, was the tragedy of Queen Gorboduc, in English verse, written by that famous Lord Buckhurst, afterwards earl of Dorset, and progenitor to that excellent person, who (as he inherits his soul and title) I wish may inherit his good fortune[1]. But, supposing our countrymen had not received this writing till of late; shall we oppose ourselves to the most polished and civilised nations of Europe? Shall we, with the same singularity, oppose the world in this, as most of us do in pronouncing Latin? Or do we desire that the brand, which Barclay has (I hope unjustly) laid upon the English, should still continue? Angli suos ac sua omnia impense mirantur; caeteras nationes despectui habent. All the Spanish and Italian tragedies, I have yet seen, are writ in rhyme. For the French, I do not name them, because it is the fate of our countrymen to admit little of theirs among us, but the basest of their men, the extravagancies of their fashions, and the frippery of their merchandise. Shakspeare (who, with some errors not to be avoided in that age, had undoubtedly a larger soul of poesy than ever any of our nation) was the first who, to shun the pains of continual rhyming, invented[A] that kind of writing which we call blank verse, but the French, more properly, prose mesuré; into which the English tongue so naturally slides, that, in writing prose, it is hardly to be avoided. And therefore, I admire some men should perpetually stumble in a way so easy, and, inverting the order of their words, constantly close their lines with verbs, which, though commended sometimes in writing Latin, yet we were whipt at Westminster if we used it twice together. I knew some, who, if they were to write in blank verse, Sir, I ask your pardon, would think it sounded more heroically to write, Sir, I your pardon ask. I should judge him to have little command of English, whom the necessity of a rhyme should force often upon this rock; though sometimes it cannot easily be avoided; and indeed this is the only inconvenience with which rhyme can be charged. This is that which makes them say, rhyme is not natural; it being only so, when the poet either makes a vicious choice of words, or places them, for rhyme sake, so unnaturally as no man would in ordinary speaking; but when it is so judiciously ordered, that the first word in the verse seems to beget the second, and that the next, till that becomes the last word in the line, which, in the negligence of prose, would be so; it must then be granted, rhyme has all the advantages of prose, besides its own. But the excellence and dignity of it were never fully known till Mr Waller taught it; he first made writing easily an art; first shewed us to conclude the sense, most commonly in distichs, which, in the verse of those before him, runs on for so many lines together, that the reader is out of breath to overtake it. This sweetness of Mr Waller's lyric poesy was afterwards followed in the epic by Sir John Denham, in his Cooper's-Hill, a poem which, your Lordship knows, for the majesty of the style, is, and ever will be, the exact standard of good writing. But if we owe the invention of it to Mr Waller, we are acknowledging for the noblest use of it to Sir William D'Avenant, who at once brought it upon the stage, and made it perfect, in the Siege of Rhodes.

[Footnote 1: The tragedy of Ferrex and Perrex (which is the proper title) was written by Thomas Sackville, Lord Buckhurst, afterwards earl of Dorset, and Thomas Norton, a barrister at law. In Sackville's part of the play, which comprehends the two last acts, there is some poetry worthy of the author of the sublime Introduction to the Mirror of Magistrates. While both the authors were out of England, one William Griffiths published a spurious copy, under the title of Gorboduc, the name of one of the principal personages, who is not, however, queen, but king, of England, But, what was a wider mistake, considering Dryden's purpose of mentioning the work, it is not written in rhyme, but in blank verse, excepting the choruses, which are in stanzas of six lines. The name of the queen is Videna. Sir Philip Sydney says, "Gorboduc is full of stately speeches and well sounding phrases, climbing up to the height of Seneca his style, and as full of notable morality, which it doth most delightfully teach, and thereby obtain the very end of poetry."]

[Footnote A: This is a mistake. Marlow, and several other dramatic authors, used blank verse before the days of Shakspeare.]

The advantages which rhyme has over blank verse are so many, that it were lost time to name them. Sir Philip Sidney, in his Defence of Poesy, gives us one, which, in my opinion, is not the least considerable; I mean the help it brings to memory, which rhyme so knits up, by the affinity of sounds, that, by remembering the last word in one line, we often call to mind both the verses. Then, in the quickness of repartees (which in discoursive scenes fall very often), it has so particular a grace, and is so aptly suited to them, that the sudden smartness of the answer, and the sweetness of the rhyme, set off the beauty of each other. But that benefit which I consider most in it, because I have not seldom found it, is, that it bounds and circumscribes the fancy. For imagination in a poet is a faculty so wild and lawless, that, like an high-ranging spaniel, it must have clogs tied to it, lest it out-run the judgment. The great easiness of blank verse renders the poet too luxuriant; he is tempted to say many things, which might better be omitted, or at least shut up in fewer words; but when the difficulty of artful rhyming is interposed, where the poet commonly confines his sense to his couplet, and must contrive that sense into such words, that the rhyme shall naturally follow them, not they the rhyme; the fancy then gives leisure to the judgment to come in, which, seeing so heavy a tax imposed, is ready to cut off all unnecessary expences. This last consideration has already answered an objection which some have made, that rhyme is only an embroidery of sense, to make that, which is ordinary in itself, pass for excellent with less examination. But certainly, that, which most regulates the fancy, and gives the judgment its busiest employment, is like to bring forth the richest and clearest thoughts. The poet examines that most, which he produceth with the greatest leisure, and which, he knows, must pass the severest test of the audience, because they are aptest to have it ever in their memory; as the stomach makes the best concoction, when it strictly embraces the nourishment, and takes account of every little particle as it passes through. But, as the best medicines may lose their virtue, by being ill applied, so is it with verse, if a fit subject be not chosen for it. Neither must the argument alone, but the characters and persons, be great and noble; otherwise, (as Scaliger says of Claudian) the poet will be ignobitiore materiâ depressus. The scenes, which, in my opinion, most commend it, are those of argumentation and discourse, on the result of which the doing or not doing some considerable action should depend.

But, my lord, though I have more to say upon this subject, yet I must remember, it is your lordship to whom I speak; who have much better commended this way by your writing in it, than I can do by writing for it. Where my reasons cannot prevail, I am sure your lordship's example must. Your rhetoric has gained my cause; at least the greatest part of my design has already succeeded to my wish, which was to interest so noble a person in the quarrel, and withal to testify to the world how happy I esteem myself in the honour of being,

MY LORD,

Your Lordship's most humble,
and most obedient servant,
JOHN DRYDEN.

PROLOGUE

'Tis much desired, you judges of the town
Would pass a vote to put all prologues down;
For who can show me, since they first were writ,

They e'er converted one hard-hearted wit?
Yet the world's mended well; in former days
Good prologues were as scarce as now good plays.
For the reforming poets of our age,
In this first charge, spend their poetic rage:
Expect no more when once the prologue's done;
The wit is ended ere the play's begun.
You now have habits, dances, scenes, and rhymes;
High language often; ay, and sense, sometimes.
As for a clear contrivance, doubt it not;
They blow out candles to give light to th' plot.
And for surprise, two bloody-minded men
Fight till they die, then rise and dance again.
Such deep intrigues you're welcome to this day:
But blame yourselves, not him who writ the play;
Though his plot's dull, as can be well desired,
Wit stiff as any you have e'er admired:
He's bound to please, not to write well; and knows,
There is a mode in plays as well as clothes;
Therefore, kind judges—

SECOND PROLOGUE enters.

SECOND PROLOGUE - Hold; would you admit
For judges all you see within the pit?

FIRST PROLOGUE - Whom would he then except, or on what score?

SECOND PROLOGUE - All, who (like him) have writ ill plays before;
For they, like thieves condemned, are hangmen made,
To execute the members of their trade.
All that are writing now he would disown,
But then he must except—even all the town;
All cholerick, losing gamesters, who, in spite,
Will damn to day, because they lost last night;
All servants, whom their mistress' scorn upbraids;
All maudlin lovers, and all slighted maids;
All, who are out of humour, or severe;
All, that want wit, or hope to find it here.

DRAMATIS PERSONAE:

DON GONSALVO DE PERALTA, a young gentleman newly arrived from the Indies, in love with JULIA.
DON RODORIGO DE SYLVA, in love with the same lady.
DON MANUEL DE TORRES, brother to JULIA.
JULIA, elder sister to DON MANUEL, promised to RODORIGO.
HONORIA, younger sister to DON MANUEL, disguised in the habit of a man, and going by the name of HIPPOLITO, in love with GONSALVO.

ANGELINA, sister to DON RODORIGO, in man's habit, likewise in love with GONSALVO, and going by the name of AMIDEO.

Servants, Robbers, Seamen, and Masquers.

This play, like "The Wild Gallant", is a drama of intrigue, borrowed from the Spanish, and claiming merit only in proportion to the diversity and ingenuity of the incidents represented. On this point every reader can decide for himself; and it would be an invidious task to point out blemishes, where, to own the truth, there are but few beauties. The ease with which the affections of almost every female in the drama are engrossed by Gonsalvo, and afterwards transferred to the lovers, upon whom the winding up of the plot made it necessary to devolve them, will, it is probable, strike every reader as unnatural. In truth, when the depraved appetite of the public requires to be gratified by trick and bustle, instead of nature and sentiment, authors must sacrifice the probable, as well as the simple, process of events.

The author seems principally to have valued himself on this piece, because it contains some scenes executed in rhyme, in what was then called the heroic manner. Upon this opinion, which Dryden lived to retract, I have ventured to offer my sentiments in the Life of the Author. In other respects, though not slow in perceiving and avouching his own merit, our author seems to consider the "Rival Ladies" as no very successful dramatic effort.

The "Rival Ladies" is supposed to have been first acted in 1663, and was certainly published in the year following. Of its success we know nothing particular. It is probable, the flowing verse, into which some part of the dialogue is thrown, with the strong point and antithesis, which distinguishes Dryden's works, and particularly his argumentative poetry, tended to redeem the credit of the author of the "Wild Gallant."

ACT I

SCENE I - A Wood.

Enter GONSALVO and a Servant.

GONSALVO - Nay, 'twas a strange as well as cruel storm,
To take us almost in the port of Sevile,
And drive us up as far as Barcelona;
The whole plate fleet was scattered, some part wrecked;
There one might see the sailors diligent
To cast o'erboard the merchant's envied wealth,
While he, all pale and dying, stood in doubt,
Whether to ease the burden of the ship,
By drowning of his ingots, or himself.

SERVANT - Fortune, sir, is a woman everywhere,
But most upon the sea.

GONSALVO - Had that been all,
I should not have complained; but, ere we could
Repair our ship, to drive us back again,

Was such a cruelty—

SERVANT - Yet that short time you staid at Barcelona
You husbanded so well, I think you left
A mistress there.

GONSALVO - I made some small essays
Of love; what might have been I cannot tell:
But, to leave that, upon what part of Spain
Are we now cast?

SERVANT - Sir, I take that city to be Alicant.

GONSALVO - Some days must of necessity be spent
In looking to our ship; then back again
For Sevile.

SERVANT - There you're sure you shall be welcome.

GONSALVO - Aye, if my brother Rodoric be returned
From Flanders; but 'tis now three years since I
Have heard from him, and, since I saw him, twelve.

SERVANT - Your growth, and your long absence in the Indies,
Have altered you so much, he'll scarcely know you.

GONSALVO - I'm sure I should not him, and less my sister;
Who, when I with my uncle went this voyage,
Was then one of those little prating girls,
Of whom fond parents tell such tedious stories:
Well, go you back.

SERVANT - I go, sir.

GONSALVO - And take care
None of the seamen slip ashore.

SERVANT - I shall, sir.

[Exit Servant.

GONSALVO - I'll walk a little while among these trees,
Now the fresh evening air blows from the hills,
And breathes the sweetness of the orange flowers
Upon me, from the gardens hear the city.

Robbers within.

1st ROBBER - I say, make sure, and kill him.

HIPPOLITO - For heaven's dear sake have pity on my youth.

[Within.

GONSALVO - Some violence is offered in the wood
By robbers to a traveller: Whoe'er
Thou art, humanity obliges me
To give thee succour.

HIPPOLITO - Help! ah cruel men! [Within.

GONSALVO - This way, I think, the voice came; 'tis not far. [Exit.

The SCENE draws, and discovers HIPPOLITO bound to a tree, and two Robbers by him with drawn swords.

2nd ROBBER - Strip him, and let him go.

1st ROBBER - Dispatch him quite; off with his doublet quickly.

HIPPOLITO - Ah me, unfortunate!

Enter GONSALVO, seizes the sword of one of them, and runs
him through; then, after a little resistance, disarms the other.

2nd ROBBER - If you have mercy in you, spare my life;
I never was consenting to a deed
So black as murder, though my fellow urged me:
I only meant to rob, and I am punished
Enough, in missing of my wicked aim.

GONSALVO - Do they rob angels here? This sweet youth has
A face so like one, which I lately saw,
It makes your crime of kin to sacrilege:
But live; and henceforth
Take nobler courses to maintain your life:
Here's something that will rescue you from want,
'Till you can find employment.
[Gives him gold, and unbinds HIPPOLITO.

HIPPOLITO - What strange adventure's this! How little hoped I,
When thus disguised I stole from Barcelona,
To be relieved by brave Gonsalvo here? [Aside.

2nd ROBBER - That life, you have preserved, shall still be yours;
And that you may perceive, how much my nature
Is wrought upon by this your generous act,
That goodness, you have shown to me, I'll use
To others for your sake, if you dare trust me
A moment from your sight.

GONSALVO - Nay, take your sword;

I will not so much crush a budding virtue,
As to suspect.

[Gives him his sword. Exit Robber.

Sweet youth, you shall not leave me,
Till I have seen you safe.

HIPPOLITO - You need not doubt it:
Alas! I find I cannot, if I would:
I am but freed to be a greater slave: [Aside.
How much am I obliged, sir, to your valour!

GONSALVO - Rather to your own sweetness, pretty youth;
You must have been some way preserved, though I
Had not been near; my aid did but prevent
Some miracle more slowly setting out
To save such excellence.

HIPPOLITO - How much more gladly could I hear those words,
If he, that spoke them, knew he spoke to me! [Aside.

Enter the Robber again with Don MANUEL, and JULIA, bound.

My brother and my sister prisoners too!
They cannot sure discover me through this
Disguise; however, I'll not venture it.
[Steps behind the trees.

2nd ROBBER - This gentleman and lady
[To GONSALVO privately.
My fellows bound.

[Exit Robber.

MANUEL - We must prepare to die;
This is the captain of the Picarons.

JULIA - Methinks he looks like one; I have a strange
Aversion to that man; he's fatal to me.

GONSALVO - I ne'er saw excellence in womankind
[Stares on her.
Till now, and yet discern it at the first:
Perfection is discovered in a moment;
He, that ne'er saw the sun before, yet knows him.

JULIA - How the villain stares upon me!

GONSALVO - Wonder prepares my soul, and then love enters:
But wonder is so close pursued by love,

That, like a fire, it warms as soon as born.

MANUEL - If we must die, what need these circumstances?

JULIA - Heaven defend me from him!

GONSALVO - Why, madam, can you doubt a rudeness from me?
Your very fears and griefs create an awe,
Such majesty they bear; methinks, I see
Your soul retired within her inmost chamber.
Like a fair mourner sit in state, with all
The silent pomp of sorrow round about her.

MANUEL - Your language does express a man, bred up
To worthier ways than those you follow now.

GONSALVO - What does he mean? [Aside.

MANUEL - If (as it seems) you love; love is a passion,
Which kindles honour into noble acts:
Restore my sister's liberty; oblige her,
And see what gratitude will work.

GONSALVO - All this is stranger yet.

MANUEL - Whate'er a brother's power
To-morrow can do for you, claim it boldly.

GONSALVO - I know not why you think yourselves my prisoners;
This lady's freedom is a thing too precious
To be disposed by any but herself:
But value this small service as you please,
Which you reward too prodigally, by
Permitting me to pay her more.

JULIA - Love from an outlaw? from a villain, love?
If I have that power on thee, thou pretend'st,
Go and pursue thy mischiefs, but presume not
To follow me:—Come, brother. [Exit Jul. and Man.

GONSALVO - Those foul names of outlaw and of villain
I never did deserve: They raise my wonder. [Walks.
Dull that I was, not to find this before!
She took me for the captain of the robbers;
It must be so; I'll tell her her mistake.

[Goes out hastily, and returns immediately.

She's gone, she's gone, and who or whence she is
I cannot tell; methinks, she should have left
A track so bright, I might have followed her;

Like setting suns, that vanish in a glory.
O villain that I am! O hated villain!

Enter HIPPOLITO again.

HIPPOLITO - I cannot suffer you to wrong yourself
So much; for, though I do not know your person,
Your actions are too fair, too noble, sir,
To merit that foul name.

GONSALVO - Pr'ythee, do not flatter me; I am a villain;
That admirable lady said I was.

HIPPOLITO - I fear, you love her, sir.

GONSALVO - No, no, not love her:
Love is the name of some more gentle passion;
Mine is a fury, grown up in a moment
To an extremity, and lasting in it;
An heap of powder set on fire, and burning
As long as any ordinary fuel.

HIPPOLITO - How could he love so soon? and yet, alas!
What cause have I to ask that question,
Who loved him the first minute that I saw him?
I cannot leave him thus, though I perceive
His heart engaged another way. [Aside.

Sir, can you have such pity on my youth, [To Him.
On my forsaken and my helpless youth,
To take me to your service?

GONSALVO - Would'st thou serve
A madman? how can he take care of thee,
Whom fortune and his reason have abandoned?
A man, that saw, and loved, and disobliged,
Is banished, and is mad, all in a moment.

HIPPOLITO - Yet you alone have title to my service;
You make me yours by your preserving me:
And that's the title heaven has to mankind.

GONSALVO - Pr'ythee, no more.

HIPPOLITO - I know your mistress too.

GONSALVO - Ha! dost thou know the person I adore?
Answer me quickly; speak, and I'll receive thee:
Hast thou no tongue?

HIPPOLITO - Why did I say I knew her?

All I can hope for, if I have my wish
To live with him, is but to be unhappy. [Aside.

GONSALVO - Thou false and lying boy, to say thou knew'st her;
Pr'ythee, say something, though thou cozen'st me.

HIPPOLITO - Since you will know, her name is Julia, sir,
And that young gentleman you saw, her brother,
Don Manuel de Torres.

GONSALVO - Say I should take thee, boy, and should employ thee
To that fair lady, would'st thou serve me faithfully?

HIPPOLITO - You ask me an hard question: I can die
For you; perhaps I cannot woo so well.

GONSALVO - I knew thou would'st not do't.

HIPPOLITO - I swear I would:
But, sir, I grieve to be the messenger
Of more unhappy news; she must be married
This day to one Don Roderick de Sylva,
Betwixt whom and her brother there has been.
A long (and it was thought a mortal) quarrel,
But now it must for ever end in peace:
For, happening both to love each others sisters,
They have concluded it in a cross marriage;
Which, in the palace of Don Rodorick,
They went to celebrate from their countryhouse,
When, taken by the thieves, you rescued them.

GONSALVO - Methinks I am grown patient on a sudden,
And all my rage is gone: like losing gamesters,
Who fret and storm, and swear at little losses;
But, when they see all hope of fortune vanished,
Submit, and gain a temper by their ruin.

HIPPOLITO - Would you could cast this love, which troubles you,
Out of your mind!

GONSALVO - I cannot, boy; but since
Her brother, with intent to cozen me,
Made me the promise of his best assistance,
I'll take some course to be revenged of him.

[Is going out.

But stay—I charge thee, boy, discover not
To any, who I am.

HIPPOLITO - Alas, I cannot, sir; I know you not.

GONSALVO - Why, there's it; I am mad again; Oh love!

HIPPOLITO - Oh love! [Exeunt.

SCENE II

Enter two Servants of Don RODORICK'S, placing chairs, and talking as they place them.

1st SERVANT - Make ready quickly there; Don Manuel
And his fair sister, that must be our lady,
Are coming in.

2nd SERVANT - They have been long expected;
'Tis evening now, and the canonic hours
For marriage are past.

1st SERVANT - The nearer bedtime,
The better still; my lord will not defer it:
He swears, the clergy are no fit judges
Of our necessities.

2nd SERVANT - Where is my lord?

1st SERVANT - Gone out to meet his bride.

2nd SERVANT - I wonder that my lady Angelina
Went not with him; she's to be married too.

1st SERVANT - I do not think she fancies much the man:
Only, to make the reconcilement perfect
Betwixt the families, she's passive in it;
The choice being but her brother's, not her own.

2nd SERVANT - Troth, were't my case, I cared not who
chose for me.

1st SERVANT - Nor I; 'twould save the process of a tedious passion,
A long law-suit of love, which quite consumes
An honest lover, ere he gets possession:
I would come plump, and fresh, and all my self,
Served up to my bride's bed like a fat fowl,
Before the frost of love had nipped me through.
I look on wives as on good dull companions,
For elder brothers to sleep out their time with;
All, we can hope for in the marriage-bed,
Is but to take our rest; and what care I,
Who lays my pillow for me?

Enter a Poet with verses.

1st SERVANT - Now, what's your business, friend?

POET - An epithalamium, to the noble bridegrooms.

1st SERVANT - Let me see; what's here? as I live,
[Takes it.
Nothing but downright bawdry: Sirrah, rascal,
Is this an age for ribaldry in verse;
When every gentleman in town speaks it
With so much better grace, than thou canst write it?
I'll beat thee with a stave of thy own rhymes.

POET - Nay, good sir—[Runs off, and Exit.

2nd SERVANT - Peace, they are here.

[Enter Don RODORICK, Don MANUEL, JULIA, and Company.

1st SERVANT - My lord looks sullenly, and fain would
hide it.

2nd SERVANT - Howe'er he weds Don Manuel's sister, yet
I fear he's hardly reconciled to him.

JULIA - I tremble at it still.

Don RODORICK - I must confess
Your danger great; but, madam, since 'tis past,
To speak of it were to renew your fears.
My noble brother, welcome to my breast.
Some, call my sister; say, Don Manuel,
Her bridegroom, waits.

MANUEL - Tell her, in both the houses
There now remains no enemy but she.

Don RODORICK - In the mean time let's dance; madam, I
hope You'll grace me with your hand—

[Enter LEONORA, woman to ANGELINA; takes the two men aside.

LEONORA - O sir, my lady Angelina—

Don RODORICK - Why comes she not?

LEONORA - Is fallen extremely sick.

Both: How?

GONSALVO - Why, there's it; I am mad again; Oh love!

HIPPOLITO - Oh love! [Exeunt.

Enter two Servants of Don RODORICK'S, placing chairs, and talking as they place them.

1st SERVANT - Make ready quickly there; Don Manuel
And his fair sister, that must be our lady,
Are coming in.

2nd SERVANT - They have been long expected;
'Tis evening now, and the canonic hours
For marriage are past.

1st SERVANT - The nearer bedtime,
The better still; my lord will not defer it:
He swears, the clergy are no fit judges
Of our necessities.

2nd SERVANT - Where is my lord?

1st SERVANT - Gone out to meet his bride.

2nd SERVANT - I wonder that my lady Angelina
Went not with him; she's to be married too.

1st SERVANT - I do not think she fancies much the man:
Only, to make the reconcilement perfect
Betwixt the families, she's passive in it;
The choice being but her brother's, not her own.

2nd SERVANT - Troth, were't my case, I cared not who
chose for me.

1st SERVANT - Nor I; 'twould save the process of a tedious passion,
A long law-suit of love, which quite consumes
An honest lover, ere he gets possession:
I would come plump, and fresh, and all my self,
Served up to my bride's bed like a fat fowl,
Before the frost of love had nipped me through.
I look on wives as on good dull companions,
For elder brothers to sleep out their time with;
All, we can hope for in the marriage-bed,
Is but to take our rest; and what care I,
Who lays my pillow for me?

Enter a Poet with verses.

1st SERVANT - Now, what's your business, friend?

POET - An epithalamium, to the noble bridegrooms.

1st SERVANT - Let me see; what's here? as I live,
[Takes it.
Nothing but downright bawdry: Sirrah, rascal,
Is this an age for ribaldry in verse;
When every gentleman in town speaks it
With so much better grace, than thou canst write it?
I'll beat thee with a stave of thy own rhymes.

POET - Nay, good sir—[Runs off, and Exit.

2nd SERVANT - Peace, they are here.

[Enter Don RODORICK, Don MANUEL, JULIA, and Company.

1st SERVANT - My lord looks sullenly, and fain would
hide it.

2nd SERVANT - Howe'er he weds Don Manuel's sister, yet
I fear he's hardly reconciled to him.

JULIA - I tremble at it still.

Don RODORICK - I must confess
Your danger great; but, madam, since 'tis past,
To speak of it were to renew your fears.
My noble brother, welcome to my breast.
Some, call my sister; say, Don Manuel,
Her bridegroom, waits.

MANUEL - Tell her, in both the houses
There now remains no enemy but she.

Don RODORICK - In the mean time let's dance; madam, I
hope You'll grace me with your hand—

[Enter LEONORA, woman to ANGELINA; takes the two men aside.

LEONORA - O sir, my lady Angelina—

Don RODORICK - Why comes she not?

LEONORA - Is fallen extremely sick.

Both: How?

LEONORA - Nay, trouble not yourselves too much;
These fits are usual with her, and not dangerous.

Don RODORICK - O rarely counterfeited.
[Aside.

MANUEL - May not I see her?

LEONORA - She does, by me, deny herself that honour.
[As she speaks, steals a note into his hand.
I shall return, I hope, with better news;
In the mean time she prays, you'll not disturb
The company.

[Exit LEONORA.

Don RODORICK - This troubles me exceedingly.

MANUEL - A note put privately into my hand
By Angelina's woman? She's my creature:
There's something in't; I'll read it to myself—
[Aside.

Don RODORICK - Brother, what paper's that?

MANUEL - Some begging verses,
Delivered me this morning on my wedding.

Don RODORICK - Pray, let me see them.

MANUEL - I have many copies,
Please you to entertain yourself with these.
[Gives him another paper. MANUEL reads.

SIR,
My lady feigns this sickness to delude you:
Her brother hates you still; and the plot is,
That he shall marry first your sister,
And then deny you his.

Yours, LEONORA.

POSTSCRIPT.

Since I writ this, I have so wrought upon her,
(Who, of herself, is timorous enough)
That she believes her brother will betray her,
Or else be forced to give her up to you;
Therefore, unknown to him, she means to fly:
Come to the garden door at seven this evening,
And there you may surprise her; mean time, I

Will keep her ignorant of all things, that
Her fear may still increase.

Enter LEONORA again.

Don RODORICK - How now? How does your lady?

LEONORA - So ill, she cannot possibly wait on you.

MANUEL - Kind heaven, give me her sickness!

Don RODORICK - Those are wishes:
What's to be done?

MANUEL - We must defer our marriages.

Don RODORICK - Leonora, now! [Aside to her

LEONORA - My lady, sir, has absolutely charged,
Her brother's should go forward.

Don RODORICK - Absolutely!

LEONORA - Expressly, sir; because, she says, there are
So many honourable persons here,
Whom to defraud of their intended mirth,
And of each others company, were rude:
So, hoping your excuse—[Exit LEONORA.

Don RODORICK - That privilege of power, which brothers have
In Spain, I never used, therefore submit
My will to hers; but with much sorrow, sir,
My happiness should go before, not wait
On yours: Lead on.

MANUEL - Stay, sir; though your fair sister, in respect
To this assembly, seems to be content
Your marriage should proceed, we must not want
So much good manners as to suffer it.

Don RODORICK - So much good manners, brother?

Manuel - I have said it.
Should we, to show our sorrow for her sickness,
Provoke our easy souls to careless mirth,
As if our drunken revels were designed
For joy of what she suffers?

Don RODORICK - 'Twill be over
In a few days.

MANUEL - Your stay will be the less.

Don RODORICK - All things are now in readiness, and must not
Be put off, for a peevish humour thus.

MANUEL - They must; or I shall think you mean not fairly.

Don RODORICK - Explain yourself.

MANUEL - That you would marry first,
And afterwards refuse me Angelina.

RODORICK - Think so.

MANUEL - You are—

Don RODORICK - Speak softly.

MANUEL - A foul villain.

Don RODORICK - Then—

MANUEL - Speak softly.

Don RODORICK - I'll find a time to tell you, you are one.

MANUEL - 'Tis well.
Ladies, you wonder at our private whispers,

[To the company.
But more will wonder when you know the cause;
The beauteous Angelina is fallen ill;
And, since she cannot with her presence grace
This day's solemnity, the noble Roderick
Thinks fit it be deferred, 'till she recover;
Then, we both hope to have your companies.

LEONORA - Wishing her health, we take our leaves.

[Exeunt company.

Don RODORICK - Your sister yet will marry me.

MANUEL - She will not: Come hither, Julia.

JULIA - What strange afflicting news is this you tell us?

MANUEL - 'Twas all this false man's plot, that when he had
Possest you, he might cheat me of his sister.

JULIA - Is this true, Roderick?   Alas, his silence

Does but too much confess it: How I blush
To own that love, I cannot yet take from thee!
Yet for my sake be friends.

MANUEL - 'Tis now too late:
I am by honour hindered.

Don RODORICK - I by hate.

JULIA - What shall I do?

MANUEL - Leave him, and come away;
Thy virtue bids thee.

JULIA - But love bids me stay.

MANUEL - Her love's so like my own, that I should blame
The brother's passion in the sister's flame.
Rodorick, we shall meet. He little thinks
I am as sure this night of Angelina,
As he of Julia. [Aside.

Exit MANUEL.

Don RODORICK - Madam, to what an ecstasy of joy
Your goodness raises me! this was an act
Of kindness, which no service e'er can pay.

JULIA - Yes, Rodorick, 'tis in your power to quit
The debt you owe me.

Don RODORICK - Do but name the way.

JULIA - Then briefly thus; 'tis to be just to me,
As I have been to you.

Don RODORICK - You cannot doubt it.

JULIA - You know I have adventured, for your sake,
A brother's anger, and the world's opinion:
I value neither; for a settled virtue
Makes itself judge, and, satisfied within,
Smiles at that common enemy, the world.
I am no more afraid of flying censures,
Than heaven of being fired with mounting sparkles.

Don RODORICK - But wherein must my gratitude consist?

JULIA - Answer yourself, by thinking what is fit
For me to do.

Don RODORICK - By marriage, to confirm
Our mutual love.

JULIA - Ungrateful Rodorick!
Canst thou name marriage, while thou entertain'st
A hatred so unjust against my brother?

Don RODORICK - But, unkind Julia, you know the causes
Of love and hate are hid deep in our stars,
And none but heaven can give account of both.

JULIA - Too well I know it: for my love to thee
Is born by inclination, not by judgment;
And makes my virtue shrink within my heart,
As loth to leave it, and as loth to mingle.

Don RODORICK - What would you have me do?

JULIA - Since I must tell thee,
Lead me to some near monastery; there
(Till heaven find out some way to make us happy)
I shall be kept in safety from my brother.

Don RODORICK - But more from me; what hopes can Rodorick
have,
That she, who leaves him freely, and unforced,
Should ever of her own accord return?

JULIA - Thou hast too great assurance of my faith,
That, in despite of my own self, I love thee.
Be friends with Manuel, I am thine; 'till when
My honour's. Lead me.

[Exeunt.

SCENE III - The representation of a Street discovered by twilight.

Enter Don MANUEL, solus.

MANUEL - This is the time and place, where I expect
My fugitive mistress; if I meet with her,
I may forget the wrongs, her brother did me;
If otherwise, his blood shall expiate them.
I hope her woman keeps her ignorant
How all things passed, according to her promise.

A door opens. Enter ANGELINA in boy's clothes.
LEONORA behind at the door.

LEONORA - I had forgot to tell him of this habit
She has put on; but sure he'll know her in it.

[Aside.

MANUEL - Who goes there?

ANGELINA - 'Tis Don Manuel's voice; I must run back:
The door shut on me?—Leonora! where?—Does
she not follow me? I am betrayed.

MANUEL - What are you?

ANGELINA - A poor boy.

MANUEL - Do you belong to Rodorick?

ANGELINA - Yes, I do.

MANUEL - Here's money for you; tell me where's his
sister?

ANGELINA - Just now I met her coming down the stairs,
Which lead into the garden.

MANUEL - 'Tis well; leave me
In silence.

ANGELINA - With all my heart; was ever such a 'scape?
[Exit running.

MANUEL - She cannot now be long; sure by the moons shine
I shall discover her:

Enter RODORICK and JULIA.

This must be she; I'll seize her.

JULIA - Help me, Roderick.

Don RODORICK - Unhand the lady, villain.

MANUEL - Roderick!
I'm glad we meet alone; now is the time
To end our difference.

Don RODORICK - I cannot stay.

MANUEL - You must.

Don RODORICK - I will not.

MANUEL - 'Tis base to injure any man; but yet
Tis far more base, once done, not to defend it.

Don RODORICK - Is this an hour, for valiant men to fight?
They love the sun should witness what they do;
Cowards have courage, when they see not death;
And fearful hares, that sculk in forms all day,
Yet fight their feeble quarrels by the moonlight.

MANUEL - No; light and darkness are but poor distinctions
Of such, whose courage comes by fits and starts.

Don RODORICK - Thou urgest me above my patience;
This minute of my life was not my own,
But hers, I love beyond it. [They draw, and fight.

JULIA - Help, help! none hear me!
Heaven, I think, is deaf too:
O Roderick! O brother!

Enter GONSALVO, and HIPPOLITO.

JULIA - Whoe'er you are, if you have honour, part
them! [MANUEL stumbles, and falls.

GONSALVO - Hold, sir, you are too cruel; he, that kills
At such advantage, fears to fight again.

[Holds Don RODORICK.

MANUEL - Cavalier, I may live to thank you for this
favour. [Rises.

Don RODORICK - I will not quit you so.

MANUEL - I'll breathe, and then—

JULIA - Is there no way to save their lives?

HIPPOLITO - Run out of sight,
If 'tis concerning you they quarrel.

[JULIA retires to a corner.

HIPPOLITO - Help, help, as you are cavaliers; the lady.
For whom you thus contend, is seized by some
Night-robbing villains.

ALL - Which way took they?

HIPPOLITO - 'Twas so dark I could not see distinctly.

Don RODORICK - Let us divide; I this way. [Exit.

GONSALVO - Down yonder street I'll take.

MANUEL - And I down that. [Exeunt severally.

HIPPOLITO - Now, madam, may we not lay by our fear?
They are all gone.

JULIA - Tis true; but we are here,
Exposed to darkness, without guide or aid,
But of ourselves.

HIPPOLITO - And of ourselves afraid.

JULIA - These dangers, while 'twas light, I could
despise;
Then I was bold, but watched by many eyes:
Ah! could not heaven for lovers find a way,
That prying people still might sleep by day?

Enter ANGELINA.

HIPPOLITO - Methinks I'm certain I discover some.

JULIA - This was your speaking of them, made them
come.

HIPPOLITO - There is but one, perhaps he may go by.

ANGELINA - Where had I courage for this bold disguise,
Which more my nature than my sex belies?
Alas! I am betrayed to darkness here;
Darkness, which virtue hates, and maids most fear:
Silence and solitude dwell every where:
Dogs cease to bark; the waves more faintly roar,
And roll themselves asleep upon the shore:
No noise but what my footsteps make, and they
Sound dreadfully, and louder than by day:
They double too, and every step I take
Sounds thick, methinks, and more than one could
make.
Ha! who are these?
I wished for company, and now I fear.
Who are you, gentle people, that go there?

JULIA - His voice is soft as is the upper air,
Or dying lovers' words: O pity us.
Ang. O pity me! take freely as your own

My gold, my jewels; spare my life alone.

HIPPOLITO - Alas, he fears as much as we.

JULIA - What say you,
Sir, will you join with us?

ANGELINA - Yes, madam; but
If you would take my sword, you'll use it better.

HIPPOLITO - Ay, but you are a man.

ANGELINA - Why, so are you.

HIPPOLITO - Truly my fear had made me quite forget it.

Enter GONSALVO.

GONSALVO - Hippolito! how barbarous was I
To leave my boy! Hippolito!

HIPPOLITO - Here, here.
Now, madam, fear not, you are safe.

JULIA - What is become, sir, of those gentlemen?

GONSALVO - Madam, they all went several ways; not like
To meet.

JULIA - What will become of me?

GONSALVO - Tis late,
And I a stranger in the town; yet all
Your dangers shall be mine.

JULIA - You're noble, sir.

GONSALVO - I'll pawn the hopes of all my love, to see
You safe.

JULIA - Whoe'er your mistress be, she has
My curses, if she prove not kind.

ANGELINA - And mine.

HIPPOLITO - My sister will repent her, when she knows
For whom she makes that wish; but I'll say nothing,
Till day discovers it. [Aside.] A door opens;
I hope it is some inn.

[A door opens, at which a Servant appears.

ANGELINA - Friend, can you lodge us here?

Serv: Yes, friend, we can.

JULIA - How shall we be disposed?

Serv: As nature would;
The gentleman and you: I have a rule,
That, when a man and woman ask for lodging,
They are ever husband and wife.

JULIA - Rude and unmannered!

GONSALVO - Sir, this lady must be lodged apart.

Serv: Then the two boys, that are good for nothing
But one another, they shall go together.

ANGELINA - Lie with a man! sweet heaven defend me!

HIPPOLITO - Alas, friend, I ever lie alone.

Serv: Then to save trouble, sir, because 'tis late,
One of the youths shall be disposed with you.

ANGELINA - Who, I! not for the world.

HIPPOLITO - Neither of us; for, though I would not lodge with you
Myself, I never can endure he should.

ANGELINA - Why then, to end the difference, if you please.
I and that lady will be bed-fellows.

HIPPOLITO - No, she and I will lodge together rather.

SERVANT - You are sweet youths indeed; not for the world
You would not lodge with men! none but the lady
Would serve your turn.

ANGELINA - Alas, I had forgot I am a boy;
I am so lately one. [Aside.

SERVANT - Well, well; all shall be lodged apart.

GONSALVO – [To HIPPOLITO I did not think you harboured wanton thoughts;
So young, so bad?

HIPPOLITO - I can make no defence,
But must be shamed by my own innocence. [Exeunt.

SCENE I - A Chamber.

[Enter GONSALVO, HIPPOLITO, and ANGELINA as AMIDEO at a distance.

GONSALVO - Hippolito, what is this pretty youth,
That follows us?

HIPPOLITO - I know not much of him:
Handsome you see, and of graceful fashion;
Of noble blood, he says, and I believe him;
But in some deep distress; he'll tell no more,
And I could cry for that, which he has told.
So much I pity him.

GONSALVO - My pretty youth,
Would I could do thee any service.

ANGELINA - Sir,
The greatest you can do me, is accepting mine.

HIPPOLITO - How's this? methinks already I begin
To hate this boy, whom but even now I moaned,
You serve my master? Do you think I cannot
Perform all duties of a servant better,
And with more care, than you?

ANGELINA - Better you may,
But never with more care:
Heaven, which is served with angels, yet admits
Poor man to pay his duty, and receives it.

HIPPOLITO - Mark but, my lord, how ill behaved a youth,
How very ugly, what a dwarf he is.

ANGELINA - My lord, I yet am young enough to grow,
And 'tis the commendation of a boy,
That he is little. [Cries.

GONSALVO - Pr'ythee, do not cry;
Hippolito, 'twas but just now you praised him,
And are you changed so soon?

HIPPOLITO - On better view.

GONSALVO - What is your name, sweet heart?

HIPPOLITO - Sweet heart! since I

Have served you, you ne'er called me so.

ANGELINA - O, ever,
Ever call me by that kind name; I'll own
No other, because I would still have that.

HIPPOLITO - He told me, sir, his name was Amideo;
Pray, call him by't.

GONSALVO - Come, I'll employ you both;
Reach me my belt, and help to put it on.

AMIDEO - I run, my lord.

HIPPOLITO - You run? it is my office.

[They both take it up, and strive for it; HIPPOLITO gets it, and puts it on.

AMIDEO - Look you, my lord, he puts it on so awkwardly;
[Crying.
The sword does not sit right.

HIPPOLITO - Why, where's the fault?

AMIDEO - I know not that; but I am sure 'tis wrong.

Gons:The fault is plain, 'tis put on the wrong shoulder.

HIPPOLITO - That cannot be, I looked on Amideo's,
And hung it on that shoulder his is on.

AMIDEO - Then I doubt mine is so.

GONSALVO - It is indeed:
You're both good boys, and both will learn in time.
Hippolito, go you and bring me word,
Whether that lady, we brought in last night,
Be willing to receive a visit from, me.

HIPPOLITO - Now, Amideo, since you are so forward
To do all service, you shall to the lady.

AMIDEO - No, I'll stay with my master, he bid you.

HIPPOLITO - It mads me to the heart to leave him here:
But I will be revenged. [Aside.
My lord, I beg
You would not trust this boy with any thing
Till my return; pray, know him better first. [Exit.

GONSALVO - 'Twas my unhappiness to meet this lady

Last night; because it ruined my design
Of walking by the house of Roderick:
Who knows but through some window I had spied
Fair Julia's shadow passing by the glass;
Or if some others, I would think it hers;
Or if not any, I would see the place
Where Julia lives. O Heaven, how small a blessing
Will serve to make despairing lovers happy!

AMIDEO - Unhappy Angelina, thou art lost:
Thy lord loves Julia. [Aside.

Enter HIPPOLITO and JULIA.

JULIA - Where is thy master?
I long to give him my acknowledgments
For my own safety, and my brother's both.
Ha! Is it he? [Looks.

GONSALVO - Can it be Julia?
Could night so far disguise her from my knowledge!

JULIA - I would not think thee him, I see thou art:
Pr'ythee disown thyself in pity to me:
Why should I be obliged by one I hate?

GONSALVO - I could say something in my own defence;
But it were half a crime to plead my cause,
When you would have me guilty.

AMIDEO - How I fear
The sweetness of those words will move her pity!
I'm sure they would do mine.

GONSALVO - You took me for a robber, but so far
I am from that—

JULIA - O, pr'ythee, be one still,
That I may know some cause for my aversion.

GONSALVO - I freed you from them, and more gladly did it—

JULIA - Be what thou wilt, 'tis now too late to tell me:
The blackness of that image, I first fancied,
Has so infected me, I still must hate thee.

HIPPOLITO - Though (if she loves him) all my hopes are ruined,
It makes me mad to see her thus unkind. [Aside.
Madam, what see you in this gentleman,
Deserves your scorn or hatred? love him, or
Expect just Heaven should strangely punish you.

GONSALVO - No more: Whate'er she does is best; and if
You would be mine, you must, like me, submit
Without dispute.

HIPPOLITO - How can I love you, sir, and suffer this?
She has forgot that, which, last night, you did
In her defence.

JULIA - O call that night again;
Pitch her with all her darkness round: then set me
In some far desert, hemmed with mountain wolves
To howl about me: This I would endure,
And more, to cancel my obligements to him.

GONSALVO - You owe me nothing, madam; if you do,
I make it void; and only ask your leave
To love you still; for, to be loved again
I never hope;

JULIA - If that will clear my debt, enjoy thy wish;
Love me, and long, and desperately love me.
I hope thou wilt, that I may plague thee more:
Mean time, take from me that detested object;
Convey thy much loathed person from my sight.

GONSALVO - Madam, you are obeyed.
Hippolito and Amideo, wait
Upon fair Julia; look upon her for me
With dying eyes, but do not speak one word
In my behalf; for, to disquiet her,
Even happiness itself were bought too dear.

[Goes farther off, towards the end of the stage.

My passion swells too high;
And, like a vessel struggling in a storm,
Requires more hands than one to steer her upright;
I'll find her brother out.

[Exit.

JULIA - That boy, I see, he trusts above the other:
He has a strange resemblance with a face
That I have seen, but when, or where, I know not.
I'll watch till they are parted; then, perhaps,
I may corrupt that little one to free me.

[Aside. Exit.

AMIDEO - Sweet Hippolito, let me speak with you.

HIPPOLITO - What would you with me?

AMIDEO - Nay, you are so fierce;
By all that's good, I love and honour you,
And, would you do but one poor thing I'll ask you,
In all things else you ever shall command me.
Look you, Hippolito, here's gold and jewels;
These may be yours.

HIPPOLITO - To what end dost thou show
These trifles to me? or how cam'st thou by them?
Not honestly, I fear.

AMIDEO - I swear I did:
And you shall have them; but you always press
Before me in my master's service so—

HIPPOLITO - And always will.

AMIDEO - But, dear Hippolito,
Why will you not give way, that I may be
First in his favour, and be still employed?
Why do you frown? 'tis not for gain I ask it;
Whatever he shall give me shall be yours,
Except it be some toy you would not care for,
Which I should keep for his dear sake, that gave it.

HIPPOLITO - If thou wouldst offer both the Indies to me,
The eastern quarries, and the western mines,
They should not buy one look, one gentle smile
Of his from me; assure thy soul they should not,
I hate thee so.

AMIDEO - Henceforth I'll hate you worse.
But yet there is a woman whom he loves,
A certain Julia, who will steal his heart
From both of us; we'll join at least against
The common enemy.

HIPPOLITO - Why does he fear my lord should love a
woman?
The passion of this boy is so like mine,
That it amazes me. [Aside.

Enter a Servant.

SERVANT - Young gentleman,
Your master calls for you.

HIPPOLITO - I'll think upon't—

[Exeunt HIPPOLITO and Servant

Enter JULIA to AMIDEO.

JULIA - Now is the time, he is alone.

AMIDEO - Here comes
The saint, my lord adores; love, pardon me
The fault, I must commit.

JULIA - Fair youth, I am
A suitor to you.

AMIDEO - So am I to you.

JULIA - You see me here a prisoner.

AMIDEO - My request
Is, I may set you free; make haste, sweet madam;
Which way would you go?

JULIA - To the next
Religious house.

AMIDEO - Here through the garden, madam;
How I commend your holy resolution! [Exeunt.

Enter DON MANUEL in the street, and a Servant
with him.

MANUEL - Angelina fled to a monastery, say you?

SERVANT - So 'tis given out: I could not see her woman:
But, for your sister, what you heard is true;
I saw her at the inn:
They told me, she was brought in late last night;
By a young cavalier, they showed me there.

MANUEL - This must be he that rescued me:
What would I give to see him!

SERVANT - Fortune is
Obedient to your wishes; he was coming
To find out you; I waited on him to
The turning of the street, and stepped before
To tell you of it.

MANUEL - You o'erjoy me.

SERVANT - This, sir, is he.

Enter GONSALVO. DON MANUEL is running to embrace him, and stops.

MANUEL - The captain of the robbers!

GONSALVO - As such, indeed, you promised me your sister.

MANUEL - I promised all the interest I should have;
Because I thought, before you came to claim it,
A husband's right would take my title from me.

GONSALVO - I come to see if any manly virtue
Can dwell with falsehood: Draw, thou'st injured me.

MANUEL - You say already I have done you wrong,
And yet would have me right you by a greater.

GONSALVO - Poor abject thing!

MANUEL - Who doubts another's courage
Wants it himself; but I, who know my own,
Will not receive a law from you to fight,
Or to forbear: for then I grant your courage
To master mine, when I am forced to do
What of myself I would not.

GONSALVO - Your reason?

MANUEL - You saved my life.

GONSALVO - I'll quit that debt, to be
In a capacity of forcing you
To keep your promise with me; for I come
To learn, your sister is not yet disposed.

MANUEL - I've lost all privilege to defend my life;
And, if you take it now, 'tis no new conquest;
Like fish, first taken in a river, then
Bestowed in ponds to catch a second time.

GONSALVO - Mark but how partially you plead your cause,
Pretending breach of honour if you fight,
Yet think it none to violate your word.

MANUEL - I cannot give my sister to a robber.

GONSALVO - You shall not; I am none, but born of blood
As noble as yourself; my fortunes equal
At least with yours, my reputation yet,
I think, unstained.

MANUEL - I wish, sir, it may prove so;
I never had so strong an inclination
To believe any man as you—But yet—

GONSALVO - All things shall be so clear, there shall be left
No room for any scruple. I was born
In Seville, of the best house in that city;
My name Gonsalvo de Peralta: Being
A younger brother, 'twas my uncle's care
To take me with him in a voyage to
The Indies, where since dying, he has left me
A fortune not contemptible; returning
From thence with all my wealth in the plate fleet,
A furious storm almost within the port
Of Seville took us, scattered all the navy.
My ship, by the unruly tempest borne
Quite through the Streights, as far as Barcelona,
There first cast anchor; there I stept ashore:
Three days I staid, in which small time I made
A little love, which vanished as it came.

MANUEL - But were you not engaged to her you
courted?

GONSALVO - Upon my honour, no; what might have been
I cannot tell: But ere I could repair
My beaten ship, or take fresh water in,
One night, when there by chance I lay aboard,
A wind tore up my anchor from the bottom,
And with that violence it brought me thither,
Has thrown me in this port.

MANUEL - But yet our meeting in the wood was strange.

GONSALVO - For that I'll satisfy you as we walk.

Enter HIPPOLITO.

HIPPOLITO - O sir, how glad am I to find you!—

[Whispers.

MANUEL - That boy I have seen somewhere, or one like him,
But where, I cannot call to mind.

HIPPOLITO - I found it out, and got before them—
And here they are—

Enter AMIDEO and JULIA.

MANUEL - My sister! as I could have wished it.

AMIDEO - O! we are caught!

JULIA - I did expect as much:
Fortune has not forgot that I am Julia.

MANUEL - Sister, I'm glad you're happily returned;
'Twas kindly done of you thus to prevent
The trouble of my search.

JULIA - I would not have you
Mistake my love to Roderick so much,
To think I meant to fall into your hands.
My purpose is for the next nunnery;
There I'll pray for you: So farewell.

MANUEL - Stay, Julia, you must go with me.

JULIA - Lead, lead;
You think I am your prisoner now.

GONSALVO - If you will needs to a religious house,
Leave that fair face behind; a worse will serve
To spoil with watching, and with fasting there.

MANUEL - Pr'ythee, no more of this; the only way
To make her happy is to force it on her.
Julia, prepare yourself strait to be married.

JULIA - To whom?

MANUEL - You see your bridegroom: And you know
My father's will, who, with his dying breath
Commanded, you should pay as strict obedience
To me, as formerly to him: If not,
Your dowry is at my dispose.

JULIA - O, would
The loss of that dispense with duty in me,
How gladly would I suffer it! and yet,
If I durst question it, methinks 'tis hard!
What right have parents over children, more
Than birds have o'er their young? yet they impose
No rich-plumed mistress on their feathered sons;
But leave their love, more open yet and free
Than all the fields of air, their spacious birthright.

[GONSALVO seems to beg MANUEL not to be harsh.

MANUEL - Nay, good Gonsalvo, trouble not yourself,
There is no other way; when 'tis once done,

She'll thank me for't.

JULIA - I ne'er expected other usage from you;
A kind brother you have been to me,
And to my sister: You have sent, they say,
To Barcelona, that my aunt should force her
To marry the old Don you brought her.

HIPPOLITO - Who could, that once had seen Gonsalvo's face?
Alas, she little thinks I am so near! [Aside.

MANUEL - Mind not what she says.
A word with you—[To GONSALVO.

AMIDEO - Don Manuel eyes me strangely; the best is,
he never saw me yet but at a distance:
My brother's jealousy (who ne'er intended
I should be his) restrained our nearer converse. [Aside.

JULIA - My pretty youth, I am enforced to trust thee
[To AMIDEO.
With my most near concerns; friends I have none,
If thou deny'st to help me.

AMIDEO - Any thing
To break your marriage with my master.

JULIA - Go to Roderick, and tell him my condition:
But tell it him as from thyself, not me.

AMIDEO - That you are forced to marry?

JULIA - But do not ask him
To succour me; if of himself he will not,
I scorn a love that must be taught its duty.

MANUEL - What youth is that? I mean the little one.

GONSALVO - I took him up last night.

MANUEL - A sweet-faced boy,
I like him strangely: Would you part with him?

AMIDEO - Alas, sir, I am good for nobody,
But for my master.

HIPPOLITO - Sir, I'll do your errand
Another time, for letting Julia go. [To AMIDEO.

MANUEL - Come, sir.

GONSALVO - I beg your pardon for a moment,
I'll but dispatch some business in my ship,
And wait you presently:

MANUEL - We'll go before;
I'll make sure Roderick shall never have her;
And 'tis at least some pleasure to destroy
His happiness, who mined first my joy.

[Exeunt all but GONSALVO; who, before he goes, whispers HIPPOLITO.

GONSALVO - Against her will fair Julia to possess,
Is not to enjoy, but ravish happiness:
Yet women pardon force, because they find
The violence of love is still most kind:
Just like the plots of well built comedies,
Which then please most, when most they do surprise:
But yet constraint love's noblest end destroys,
Whose highest joy is in another's joys:
Where passion rules, how weak does reason prove!
I yield my cause, but cannot yield my love. [Exit.

ACT III

SCENE I - A great room in DON MANUEL'S house.

HIPPOLITO solus.

My master bid me speak for him to Julia:
Hard fate, that I am made a confident
Against myself!
Yet, though unwillingly I took the office,
I would perform it well: But how can I
Prove lucky to his love, who to my own
Am so unfortunate? he trusts his passion
Like him, that ventures all his stock at once
On an unlucky hand.

Enter AMIDEO.

AMIDEO - Where is the lady Julia?

HIPPOLITO - What new treason
Against my master's love have you contrived
With her?

AMIDEO - I shall not render you account.

Enter JULIA.

JULIA - I sent for him; yet if he comes, there's danger;
Yet if he does not, I for ever lose him.
What can I wish? and yet I wish him here,
Only to take the care of me from me.
Weary with sitting out a losing hand,
Twill be some ease to see another play it.
Yesterday I refused to marry him,
To-day I run into his arms unasked;
Like a mild prince encroached upon by rebels,
Love yielded much, till honour asked for all.
How now, where's Roderick? [Sees AMIDEO.
I mean Gonsalvo. [Sees HIPPOLITO.

HIPPOLITO - You would do well to meet him—

AMIDEO - Meet him! you shall not do't: I'll throw myself,
Like a young fawning spaniel, in your way
So often, you shall never move a step,
But you shall tread on me.

JULIA - You need not beg me:
I would as soon meet a syren, as see him.

HIPPOLITO - His sweetness for those frowns no subject finds:
Seas are the field of combat for the winds:
But when they sweep along some flowery coast,
Their wings move mildly, and their rage is lost.

JULIA - 'Tis that which makes me more unfortunate;
Because his sweetness must upbraid my hate.
The wounds of fortune touch me not so near;
I can my fate, but not his virtue, bear.
For my disdain with my esteem is raised;
He most is hated when he most is praised:
Such an esteem, as like a storm appears,
Which rises but to shipwreck what it bears.

HIPPOLITO - Infection dwells upon my kindness, sure,
Since it destroys even those whom it would cure.

[Cries, and exit.

AMIDEO - Still weep, Hippolito; to me thy tears
Are sovereign, as those drops the balm-tree sweats.
But, madam, are you sure you shall not love him?
I still fear.

JULIA - Thy fear will never let thee be a man.

AMIDEO - Indeed I think it won't.

JULIA - We are now
Alone; what news from Roderick?

AMIDEO - Madam, he begs you not to fear; he has
A way, which, when you think all desperate,
Will set you free.

JULIA - If not, I will not live
A moment after it.

AMIDEO - Why? there's some comfort.

JULIA - I strongly wish, for what I faintly hope:
Like the day-dreams of melancholy men,
I think and think on things impossible,
Yet love to wander in that golden maze.

Enter DON MANUEL, HIPPOLITO, and company.

AMIDEO - Madam, your brother's here.

MANUEL - Where is the bridegroom?

HIPPOLITO - Not yet returned, sir, from his ship.

MANUEL - Sister, all this good company is met,
To give you joy.

JULIA - While I am compassed round
With mirth, my soul lies hid in shades of grief,
Whence, like the bird of night, with half shut eyes,
She peeps, and sickens at the sight of day. [Aside.

Enter Servant.

SERVANT - Sir, some gentlemen and ladies are without,
Who, to do honour to this wedding, come
To present a masque.

MANUEL - Tis well; desire them
They would leave put the words, and fall to dancing.
The poetry of the foot takes most of late.

SERVANT - The poet, sir, will take that very ill;
He's at the door, with the argument o'the masque
In verse.

MANUEL - Which of the wits is it that made it?

SERVANT - None of the wits, sir; 'tis one of the poets.

MANUEL - What subject has he chose?

SERVANT - The rape of Proserpine.

Enter GONSALVO.

MANUEL - Welcome, welcome, you have been long expected.

GONSALVO - I staid to see the unlading of some rarities,
Which are within—
Madam, your pardon that I was so long absent.

JULIA - You need not ask it for your absence, sir.

GONSALVO - Still cruel, Julia?

JULIA - The danger's here, and Roderick not here:
I am not grieved to die; but I am grieved
To think him false. [Aside.

MANUEL - Bid him begin. [The music plays.

A Cupid descends in swift motion, and speaks these verses.

CUPID - Thy conquests, Proserpine, have stretched too far;
Amidst heavens peace thy beauty makes a war:
For when, last night, I to Jove's palace went,
(The brightest part of all the firmament)
Instead of all those gods, whose thick resort
Filled up the presence of the thunderers court;
There Jove and Juno all forsaken sate,
Pensive, like kings in their declining state:
Yet (wanting power) they would preserve the show,
By hearing prayers from some few men below:
Mortals to Jove may their devotions pay;
The gods themselves to Proserpine do pray.
To Sicily the rival powers resort;
'Tis Heaven wherever Ceres keeps her court.
Phoebus and Mercury are both at strife,
The courtliest of our gods who want a wife.
But Venus, whate'er kindness she pretends,
Yet (like all females envious of their friends),
Has, by my aid, contrived a black design,
The god of hell should ravish Proserpine:
Beauties, beware; Venus will never bear
Another Venus shining in her sphere.

After Cupid's speech, Venus and Ceres descend in the slow machines; Ceres drawn by dragons, Venus by swans.

After them Phoebus and Mercury descend in swift motion. Then Cupid turns to Julia, and speaks.

CUPID - The rival deities are come to woo
A Proserpine, who must be found below:
Would you, fair nymph, become, this happy hour,
In name a goddess, as you are in power?
Then to this change the king of shades will owe
A fairer Proserpine than heaven can show.

[Julia, first whispered by AMIDEO, goes into the dance, performed by Cupid, Phoebus, Mercury, Ceres, Venus, and JULIA. Towards the end of the dance, RODORICK, in the habit of Pluto, rises from below in a black chariot, all flaming, and drawn by black horses; he ravishes Julia, who personated Proserpine, and as he is carrying her away, his vizard fails off: HIPPOLITO first discovers him.

HIPPOLITO - A rape, a rape! 'tis Roderick, 'tis Roderick!

Don RODORICK - Then I must have recourse to this. [Draws.

JULIA - O heavens!

[DON MANUEL and GONSALVO draw, and a Servant; the two that acted Phoebus and Mercury return to assist RODORICK, and are beat back by MANUEL and a Servant, while GONSALVO attacks RODORICK.

GONSALVO - Unloose thy hold, foul villain.

Don RODORICK - No, I'll grasp her
Even after death.

JULIA - Spare him, or I'll die with him.

GONSALVO - Must ravishers and villains live, while I
In vain implore her mercy?

[Thrusts at him, and hurts JULIA in the arm.

JULIA - Oh, I am murdered!

GONSALVO - Wretched that I am,
What have I done? To what strange punishment
Will you condemn this guilty hand? And yet
My eyes were guilty first—For they could look
On nothing else but you; and my unlucky hand
Too closely followed them!—

Enter MANUEL again.

MANUEL - The powers above are just, that thou still livest,
For me to kill.

Don RODORICK - You'll find no easy task on't

Alone; come both together, I defy you!
Curse on this disguise, that has betrayed me
Thus cheaply to my death.

MANUEL - Under a devil's shape, thou could'st not be
Disguised.

JULIA - Then, must he die?—
Yet, I'll not bid my Roderick farewell;
For they take leave, who mean to be long absent.

GONSALVO - Hold, sir! I have had blood enough already;
And must not murder Julia again
In him she loves. Live, sir; and thank this lady.

Don RODORICK - Take my life, and spare my thanks.

MANUEL - Though you
Forgive him, let me take my just revenge.

GONSALVO - Leave that distinction to our dull divines:
That ill, I suffer to be done, I do.

HIPPOLITO - My heart bleeds for him: to see his virtue
O'ercome so fatally, against such odds
Of fortune, and of love!—

MANUEL - Permit his death, and Julia will be yours.

JULIA - Permit it not, and Julia will thank you.

GONSALVO - Who e'er could think, that one kind word from Julia
Should be preferred to Julia herself?
Could any man think it a greater good
To save a rival, than possess a mistress?
Yet this I do! these are thy riddles, love!—
What fortune gives me, I myself destroy;
And feed my virtue, but to starve my joy.
Honour sits on me like some heavy armour,
And with its stiff defence, encumbers me;
And yet, when I would put it off, it sticks
Like Hercules's shirt; heats me at once;
And poisons me!

MANUEL - I find myself grow calm by thy example;
My panting heart heaves less and less, each pulse;
And all the boiling spirits scatter from it.
Since thou desirest he should not die, he shall not,
'Till I on nobler terms can take his life.

Don RODORICK - The next turn may be yours. Remember,

I owed this danger to your wilfulness:
Once, you might easily have been mine, and would not.

[Exit RODORICK.

MANUEL - Lead out my sister, friend; her hurt's so small,
'Twill scarce disturb the ceremony.
Ladies, once more your pardons.

[Leads out the Company. Exeunt.

Manent JULIA, GONSALVO, AMIDEO, and HIPPOLITO. GONSALVO offers his hand,
JULIA pulls back hers.

JULIA - This hand would rise in blisters, should'st thou touch it!—
My Roderick's displeased with me, and thou,
Unlucky man, the cause. Dare not so much
As once to follow me. [Exit JULIA.

GONSALVO - Not follow her! Alas, she need not bid me!
Oh, how could I presume to take that hand,
To which mine proved so fatal!
Nay, if I might, should I not fear to touch it?—
murderer's touch would make it bleed afresh!

AMIDEO - I think, sir, I could kill her for your sake.

GONSALVO - Repent that word, or I shall hate thee
Strangely: Harsh words from her, like blows from angry kings,
Though they are meant affronts, are construed favours.

HIPPOLITO - Her inclinations and aversions
Are both alike unjust; and both, I hope,
Too violent to last: Chear up yourself;
for if I live, (I hope I shall not long) [Aside.
She shall be yours.

AMIDEO - 'Twere much more noble in him,
To make a conquest of himself, than her.
She ne'er can merit him; and, hadst not thou
A mean low soul, thou wouldst not name her to him.

HIPPOLITO - Poor child, who would'st be wise above thy years!
Why dost thou talk, like a philosopher,
Of conquering love, who art not yet grown up,
To try the force of any manly passion?
The sweetness of thy mother's milk is yet
Within thy veins, not soured and turned by love.

GONSALVO - Thou hast not field enough in thy young breast,
To entertain such storms to struggle in.

AMIDEO - Young as I am, I know the power of love;
Its less disquiets, and its greater cares,
And all that's in it, but the happiness.
Trust a boy's word, sir, if you please, and take
My innocence for wisdom; Leave this lady;
Cease to persuade yourself you are in love,
And you will soon be freed. Not that I wish
A thing, so noble as your passion, lost
To all the sex: Bestow it on some other;
You'll find many as fair, though none so cruel.
Would I could be a lady for your sake!

HIPPOLITO - If I could be a woman, with a wish,
You should not be without a rival long.

AMIDEO - A cedar, of your stature, would not cause
Much jealousy.

HIPPOLITO - More than a shrub of yours.

GONSALVO - How eagerly these boys fall out for nothing!—
Tell me, Hippolito, wert thou a woman,
Who would'st thou be?

HIPPOLITO - I would be Julia, sir,
Because you love her.

AMIDEO - I would not be she,
Because she loves not you.

HIPPOLITO - True, Amideo;
And, therefore, I would wish myself a lady,
Who, I am sure, does infinitely love him.

AMIDEO - I hope that lady has a name?

HIPPOLITO - She has:
And she is called Honoria, sister to
This Julia, and bred up at Barcelona;
Who loves him with a flame so pure and noble,
That, did she know his love to Julia,
She would beg Julia to make him happy.

GONSALVO - This startles me!

AMIDEO - Oh, sir, believe him not:
They love not truly, who, on any terms,
Can part with what they love.

GONSALVO - I saw a lady

At Barcelona, of what name I know not,
Who, next to Julia, was the fairest creature
My eyes did e'er behold: But, how camest thou
To know her?

HIPPOLITO - Sir, some other time I'll tell you.

AMIDEO - It could not be Honoria, whom you saw;
For, sir, she has a face so very ugly,
That, if she were a saint for holiness,
Yet no man would seek virtue there.

HIPPOLITO - This is the lyingest boy, sir;—I am sure
He never saw Honoria; for her face,
'Tis not so bad to frighten any man—
None of the wits have libelled it.

AMIDEO - Don Roderick's sister, Angelina, does
So far exceed her, in the ornaments
Of wit and beauty, though now hid from sight,
That, like the sun, (even when eclipsed) she casts
A yellowness upon all other faces.

HIPPOLITO - I'll not say much of her, but only this,
Don Manuel saw not with my eyes, if e'er
He loved that Flanders shape; that lump of earth,
And phlegm together.

AMIDEO - You have often seen her,
It seems, by your description of her person:
But I'll maintain on any Spanish ground,
Whate'er she be, yet she is far more worthy
To have my lord her servant, than Honoria.

HIPPOLITO - And I'll maintain Honoria's right against her,
In any part of all the world.

GONSALVO - You go
Too far, to quarrel on so slight a ground.

HIPPOLITO - O pardon me, my lord, it is not slight:
I must confess, I am so much concerned,
I shall not bear it long.

AMIDEO - Nor I, assure you.

GONSALVO - I will believe what both of you have said,
That Honoria, and Angelina,
Both equally are fair.

AMIDEO - Why did you name

Honoria first?

GONSALVO - And, since you take their parts so eagerly
Henceforth I'll call you by those ladies' names:
You, my Hippolito, shall be Honoria;
And you, my Amideo, Angelina.

AMIDEO - Then all my services, I wish, may make
You kind to Angelina, for my sake.

HIPPOLITO - Put all my merits on Honoria's score,
And think no maid could ever love you more.

[Exeunt.

ACT IV

SCENE I

MANUEL solus.

MANUEL - Thus I provide for others' happiness,
And lose my own. 'Tis true, I cannot blame
Thy hatred, Angelina, but thy silence.
Thy brother's hatred made thine just; but yet
'Twas cruel in thee not to tell me so.
Conquest is noble, when an heart stands out;
But mine, which yielded, how could'st thou betray?
That heart, of which thou could'st not be deprived
By any force or power, beside thy own;
Like empires, to that fatal height arrived,
They must be ruined by themselves alone.
My guarded freedom cannot be a prize
To any scornful face a second time;
For thy idea, like a ghost, would rise,
And fright my thoughts from such another crime.

Enter a Servant, with a letter.

MANUEL - From whom?

SERVANT - Sir, the contents will soon resolve you.

[He reads.

MANUEL - Tell Roderick, he has prevented me
In my design of sending to him first.
I'll meet him, single, at the time and place;
But, for my friend, tell him, he must excuse me:

I'll hazard no man in my quarrel, but
Myself alone. [Exit Servant.
Who's within there?

Enter a Servant.

Go, call my sister, and Gonsalvo, hither.
[Exit Servant.
'Twas pushed so far, that, like two armies, we
Were drawn so closely up, we could not part
Without engagement. But they must not know it.

Enter JULIA, GONSALVO, and AMIDEO.

I have some business calls me hence, and know not
When I shall return: But, ere I go,
That power I have, by my dead father's will,
Over my sister, I bequeath to you: [To GONS.
She, and her fortunes, both be firmly yours;
And this when I revoke, let cowardice
Blast all my youth, and treason taint my age.

GONSALVO - Sir—

MANUEL - Nay, good, no thanks; I cannot stay—

[Exit MANUEL.

GONSALVO - There's something more than ordinary in this;
Go, Amideo, quickly follow him,
And bring me word which way he takes.

AMIDEO - I go, sir. [Exit AMID. JULIA kneels.

GONSALVO - Madam, when you implore the powers divine,
You have no prayers in which I will not join,
Though made against myself. [Kneels with her.

JULIA - In vain I sue,
Unless my vows may be conveyed by you.

GONSALVO - Conveyed by me! My ill success in love
Shews me, too sure, I have few friends above.
How can you fear your just desires to want?
When the gods pray, they both request and grant.

JULIA - Heaven has resigned my fortune to your hand,
If you, like heaven, the afflicted understand.

GONSALVO - The language of the afflicted is not new;
Too well I learned it, when I first saw you.

JULIA - In spite of me, you now command my fate;
And yet the vanquished seeks the victor's hate;
Even in this low submission, I declare,
That, had I power, I would renew the war.
I'm forced to stoop, and 'twere too great a blow
To bend my pride, and to deny me too.

GONSALVO - You have my heart; dispose it to your will;
If not, you know the way to use it ill.

JULIA - Cruel to me, though kind to your desert,
My brother gives my person, not my heart;
And I have left no other means to sue,
But to you only, to be freed from you.

GONSALVO - From such a suit how can you hope success,
Which, given, destroys the giver's happiness?

JULIA - You think it equal you should not resign
That power you have, yet will not leave me mine;
Yet on my will I have the power alone,
And, since you cannot move it, move your own.
Your worth and virtue my esteem may win,
But women's passions from themselves begin;
Merit may be, but force still is, in vain.

GONSALVO - I would but love you, not your love constrain;
And though your brother left me to command,
He placed his thunder in a gentle hand.

JULIA - Your favour from constraint has set me free,
But that secures not my felicity;
Slaves, who, before, did cruel masters serve,
May fly to deserts, and in freedom starve.
The noblest part of liberty they lose,
Who can but shun, and want the power to chuse.

GONSALVO - O whither would your fatal reasons move!
You court my kindness, to destroy my love.

JULIA - You have the power to make my happiness,
By giving that, which you can ne'er possess.

GONSALVO - Give you to Roderick? there wanted yet
That curse, to make my miseries complete.

JULIA - Departing misers bear a nobler mind;
They, when they can enjoy no more, are kind;
You, when your love is dying in despair,
Yet want the charity to make an heir.

GONSALVO - Though hope be dying, yet it is not dead;
And dying people with small food are fed.

JULIA - The greatest kindness dying friends can have,
Is to dispatch them, when we cannot save.

GONSALVO - Those dying people, could they speak' at all,
That pity of their friends would murder call:
For men with horror dissolution meet;
The minutes even of painful life are sweet.

JULIA - But I'm by powerful inclination led;
And streams turn seldom to their fountain head.

GONSALVO - No; 'tis a tide which carries you away;
And tides may turn, though they can never stay.

JULIA - Can you pretend to love, and see my grief
Caused by yourself, yet give me no relief?

GONSALVO - Where's my reward?

JULIA - The honour of the flame.

GONSALVO - I lose the substance, then, to gain the name.

JULIA - I do too much mistress' power betray;
Must slaves be won by courtship to obey?
Thy disobedience does to treason rise,
Which thou, like rebels, would'st with love disguise.
I'll kill myself, and, if thou can'st deny
To see me happy, thou shalt see me die.

GONSALVO - O stay! I can with less regret bequeath
My love to Roderick, than you to death:
And yet—

JULIA - What new objection can you find?

GONSALVO - But are you sure you never shall be kind?

JULIA - Never.

GONSALVO - What! never?

JULIA - Never to remove.

GONSALVO - Oh fatal never to souls damned in love!

JULIA - Lead me to Roderick.

GONSALVO - If it must be so—

JULIA - Here, take my hand, swear on it thou wilt go.

GONSALVO - Oh balmy sweetness! but 'tis lost to me,
[He kisses her hand.
Like food upon a wretch condemned to die:
Another, and I vow to go:—Once more;
If I swear often, I shall be foreswore.
Others against their wills may haste their fate;
I only toil to be unfortunate:
More my own foe than all my stars could prove;
They give her person, but I give her love.
I must not trust myself—Hippolito!

Enter HIPPOLITO.

HIPPOLITO - My lord!

GONSALVO - Quickly go find Don Roderick out:
Tell him, the lady Julia will be walking
On the broad rock, that lies beside the port,
And there expects to see him instantly.
In the mean time I'll call for Amideo.

JULIA - You'll keep your promise to Don Roderick?

GONSALVO - Madam, since you bring death, I welcome it;
But to his fortune, not his love, submit.

[Exit GONSALVO.

HIPPOLITO - I dare not ask what I too fain would hear:
But, like a tender mother, hope and fear,
My equal twins, my equal care I make,
And keep hope quiet, lest that fear should wake.
[Aside.

Exit HIPPOLITO.

JULIA - So, now I'm firmly at my own dispose;
And all the lets, my virtue caused, removed:
Now, Roderick, I come—

Enter GONSALVO again.

GONSALVO - Madam, my boy's not yet returned.

JULIA - No matter, we'll not stay for him.

GONSALVO - Pray make not too much haste.

[Exeunt JULIA and GONSALVO.

Enter DON RODORICK, and a Servant.

Don RODORICK - Have you bespoke a vessel, as I bid you?

SERVANT - I have done better; for I have employed
Some, whom I know, this day to seize a ship;
Which they have done, clapping the men within her
All under hatches, with such speed and silence,
That, though she rides at anchor in the port
Among the rest, the change is not discovered.

Don RODORICK - Let my best goods and jewels be embarked
With secrecy: We'll put to sea this night.
Have you yet found my sister, or her woman?

SERVANT - Neither, sir; but in all probability
She is with Manuel.

Don RODORICK - Would God the meanest man in Alicant
Had Angelina, rather than Don Manuel!
I never can forgive, much less forget,
How he (the younger soldier) was preferred
To that command of horse, which was my due.

SERVANT - And, after that, by force disseized you of
Your quarters—

Don RODORICK - Should I meet him seven years hence
At the altar, I would kill him there:—I had
Forgot to tell you, the design we had,
To carry Julia by force away,
Will now be needless: she'll come to the rock
To see me; you, unseen, shall stand behind,
And carry her into the vessel.

SERVANT - Shall I not help you to dispatch Don Manuel?

Don RODORICK - I neither doubt my valour nor my fortune:
But if I die, revenge me: Presently
About your business; I must to the rock,
For fear I come too late. [Exeunt severally.

SCENE III - Through a rock is discovered a navy of ships riding at a distance.

Enter AMIDEO.

AMIDEO - Thus far, unseen by Manuel, I have traced him;
He can be gone no farther than the walk
Behind the rock: I'll back, and tell my master.

Enter HIPPOLITO at the other end.

HIPPOLITO - This is the place, where Roderick must expect
His Julia:—How! Amideo here!

AMIDEO - Hippolito!

HIPPOLITO - This were so fit a time
For my revenge, had I the courage, now!
My heart swells at him, and my breath grows short;
But whether fear or anger choaks it up,
I cannot tell.

AMIDEO - He looks so ghastfully,
Would I were past him; yet I fear to try it,
Because my mind misgives me he will stop me.
By your leave, Hippolito.

HIPPOLITO - Whither so fast?

AMIDEO - You'll not presume to hinder my lord's business?
He shall know it.

HIPPOLITO - I'll make you sure, before,
For telling any tales: Do you remember,
Since you defended Angelina's beauty
Against Honoria's; nay, and would maintain it.

AMIDEO - And so I will do still; (I must feign courage,
There is no other way.) [Aside.

HIPPOLITO - I'll so revenge
That injury! (if my heart fails me not.)

AMIDEO - Come, confess truly, for, I know, it fails you.
What would you give to avoid fighting now?

HIPPOLITO - No, 'tis your heart that fails.

AMIDEO - I scorn the danger;
Yet, what compassion on your youth might do,
I cannot tell; and, therefore, do not work

Upon my pity; for I feel already
My stout heart melts.

HIPPOLITO - Oh! Are you thereabout?
Now I am sure you fear; and you shall fight.

AMIDEO - I will not fight.

HIPPOLITO - Confess, then, Angelina
Is not so fair as is Honoria.

AMIDEO - I do confess; now are you satisfied?

HIPPOLITO - There's more behind; confess her not so worthy
To be beloved, nor to possess Gonsalvo,
As fair Honoria is.

AMIDEO - That's somewhat hard.

HIPPOLITO - But you must do't, or die.

AMIDEO - Well, life is sweet;
She's not so worthy: Now, let me be gone.

HIPPOLITO - No, never to my master; swear to quit
His service, and no more to see his face.

AMIDEO - I fain would save my life, but that, which you
Propose, is but another name to die.
I cannot live without my master's sight.

HIPPOLITO - Then you must fight with me for him.

AMIDEO - I would
Do any thing with you, but fighting for him.

HIPPOLITO - Nothing but that will serve.

AMIDEO - Lay by our swords,
And I'll scratch with you for him.

HIPPOLITO - That's not manly.

AMIDEO - Well, since it must be so, I'll fight:—Unbutton.

[HIPPOLITO unbuttons slowly.

How many buttons has he? I'll be one
Behind him still. [Aside.

[Unbuttons one by one after him. HIPPOLITO makes more haste.

You are so prodigal! if you loved my master,
You would not tear his doublet so:—How's this!
Two swelling breasts! a woman, and my rival!
The stings of jealousy have given me courage,
Which nature never gave me:
Come on, thou vile dissembler of thy sex;
Expect no mercy; either thou or I
Must die upon this spot: Now for Gonsalvo—
Sa—Sa—

HIPPOLITO - This courage is not counterfeit; ah me!
What shall I do? for pity, gentle boy—

AMIDEO - No pity; such a cause as ours
Can neither give nor take it: If thou yieldest,
I will not spare thee; therefore, fight it out.
[Tears open his doublet.

HIPPOLITO - Death to my hopes! a woman! and so rare
A beauty, that my lord must needs doat on her.
I should myself, if I had been a man:
But, as I am, her eyes shoot death at me.

AMIDEO - Come, have you said your prayers?

HIPPOLITO - For thy confusion,—
Thou ravenous harpy, with an angel's face,—
Thou art discovered, thou too charming rival;
I'll be revenged upon those fatal eyes.

AMIDEO - I'll tear out thine.

HIPPOLITO - I'll bite out hungry morsels
From those plump cheeks, but I will make them
thinner.

AMIDEO - I'd beat thee to the blackness of a Moor.
But that the features of thy face are such,
Such damnable, invincible good features,
That as an Ethiop thou would'st still be loved.

HIPPOLITO - I'll quite unbend that black bow o'er thine eyes;
I'll murder thee, and Julia shall have him,
Rather than thou.

AMIDEO - I'll kill both thee and her,
Rather than any one but I shall have him.

HIPPOLITO - Come on, thou witch.

AMIDEO - Have at thy heart, thou Syren.

[They draw and fight awkwardly, not coming near one another.

AMIDEO - I think I paid you there.

HIPPOLITO - O stay a little,
And tell me in what corner of thy heart
Gonsalvo lies, that I may spare that place.

AMIDEO - He lies in the last drop of all my blood,
And never will come out, but with my soul.

HIPPOLITO - Come, come, we dally;
Would one of us were dead, no matter which!
[They fight nearer.

Enter Don MANUEL.

MANUEL - The pretty boys, that serve Gonsalvo, fighting!
I come in time to save the life of one.

[HIPPOLITO gets AMIDEO down in closing: MANUEL takes away their swords.

HIPPOLITO - For goodness' sake, hinder not my revenge.

AMIDEO - The noble Manuel has saved my life:
Heavens, how unjustly have I hated him. [Aside.

MANUEL - What is it, gentle youths, that moves you thus?
I cannot tell what causes you may find;
But, trust me, all the world, in so much sweetness,
Would be to seek where to begin a quarrel:
You seem the little Cupids in the song,
Contending for the honey-bag.

HIPPOLITO - 'Tis well
You're come; you may prevent a greater mischief:
Here 'tis Gonsalvo has appointed Roderick—

MANUEL - To fight?

HIPPOLITO - What's worse: to give your sister to him.
Won by her tears, he means to leave her free,
And to redeem her misery with his:
At least so I conjecture.

MANUEL - 'Tis a doubtful
Problem; either he loves her violently,
Or not at all.

AMIDEO - You have betrayed my master:—

[To HIPPOLITO. Aside.

HIPPOLITO - If I have injured you, I mean to give you
The satisfaction of a gentlewoman.

Enter GONSALVO and JULIA.

MANUEL - Oh, they are here; now I shall be resolved.

JULIA - My brother Manuel! what fortune's this!

MANUEL - I'm glad I have prevented you.

GONSALVO - With what
Variety my fate torments me still!
Never was man so dragged along by virtue;
But I must follow her.

JULIA - Noble Gonsalvo,
Protect me from my brother.

GONSALVO - Tell me, sir,
When you bestowed your sister on me, did not
You give her freely up to my dispose?

MANUEL - 'Tis true, I did; but never with intent
You should restore her to my enemy.

GONSALVO - 'Tis past; 'tis done: She undermined my soul
With tears; as banks are sapped away by streams.

MANUEL - I wonder what strange blessing she expects
From the harsh nature of this Rodorick;
A man made up of malice and revenge.

JULIA - If I possess him, I may be unhappy;
But if I lose him, I am surely so.
Had you a friend so desperately sick,
That all physicians had forsook his cure;
All scorched without, and all parched up within,
The moisture that maintained consuming nature
Licked up, and in a fever fried away;
Could you behold him beg, with dying eyes,
A glass of water, and refuse it him,
Because you knew it ill for his disease?
When he would die without it, how could you
Deny to make his death more easy to him?

MANUEL - Talk not to me of love, when honour suffers.

The boys will hiss at me.

GONSALVO - I suffer most:
Had there been 'choice, what would I not have chose?
To save my honour I my love must lose:
But promises, once made, are past debate,
And truth's of more necessity than fate.

MANUEL - I scarce can think your promise absolute;
There might some way be thought on, if you would,
To keep both her and it.

GONSALVO - No, no; my promise was no trick of state:
I meant to be made truly wretched first,
And then to die; and I'll perform them both.

MANUEL - Then that revenge, I meant on Rodorick,
I'll take on you. [Draws.

GONSALVO - I draw with such regret,
As merchants throw their wealth into the sea,
To save their sinking vessels from a wreck.

MANUEL - I find I cannot lift my hand against thee:
Do what thou wilt; but let not me behold it.
[Goes off a little way.
I'll cut this gordian knot I cannot loose:
To keep his promise, Rodorick shall have her,
But I'll return and rescue her by force;
Then giving back what he so frankly gave,
At once my honour and his love I'll save.

[Exit MANUEL.

Enter Don RODORICK.

Don RODORICK - How! Julia brought by him?
Who sent for me?

GONSALVO - 'Twas I.

Don RODORICK - I know your business then; 'tis fighting.

GONSALVO - You're mistaken; 'tis something that I fear.

Don RODORICK - What is't?

GONSALVO - Why,—'twill not out: Here, take her;
And deserve her: but no thanks;
For fear I should consider what I give,
And call it back.

JULIA - O my dear Rodorick!

GONSALVO - O cruel Julia!
For pity shew not all your joy before me;
Stifle some part of it one minute longer,
'Till I am dead.

JULIA - My Rodorick shall know,
He owes his Julia to you; thank him, love;
In faith I take it ill you are so slow.

Don RODORICK - You know he has forbid me; and, beside,
He'll take it better from your mouth than mine;
All that you do must needs be pleasing to him.

JULIA - Still sullen and unkind!

Don RODORICK - Why, then, in short,
I do not understand the benefit.

GONSALVO - Not to have Julia in thy free possession?

Don RODORICK - Not brought by you; not of another's leaving.

JULIA - Speak softly, Rodorick: Let not these hear thee;
But spare my shame for the ill choice I made,
In loving thee.

Don RODORICK - I will speak loud, and tell thee,
Thou com'st, all cloyed and tired with his embraces,
To proffer thy palled love to me; his kisses
Do yet bedew thy lips; the very print,
His arms made round thy body, yet remains.

GONSALVO - O barbarous jealousy!

JULIA - 'Tis an harsh word:
I am too pure for thee; but yet I love thee.

[Offers to take his hand.

Don RODORICK - Away, foul impudence.

GONSALVO - Madam, you wrong
Your virtue, thus to clear it by submission.

JULIA - Whence grows this boldness, sir? did I ask you
To be my champion?

Don RODORICK - He chose to be your friend, and not your husband:

Left that dull part of dignity to me;
As often the worst actors play the kings.

JULIA - This jealousy is but excess of passion,
Which grows up, wild, in every lover's breast;
But changes kind when planted in an husband.

Don RODORICK - Well, what I am, I am; and what I will be,
When you are mine, my pleasure shall determine.
I will receive no law from any man.

JULIA - This strange unkindness of my Rodorick
I owe to thee, and thy unlucky love;
Henceforth go lock it up within thy breast;
'Tis only harmless while it is concealed,
But, opened, spreads infection like a vault.
Go, and my curse go with thee!—

GONSALVO - I cannot go 'till I behold you happy:—
Here, Rodorick, receive her on thy knees;
Use her with that respect, which thou would'st pay
Thy guardian angel, if he could be seen.
Do not provoke my anger by refusing.
I'll watch thy least offence to her; each word,
Nay, every sullen look;—
And, as the devils, who are damned to torments,
Yet have the guilty souls their slaves to punish;
So, under me, while I am wretched, thou
Shalt be tormented.

Don RODORICK - Would'st thou make me the tenant of thy lust,
To toil, and for my labour take the dregs,
The juicy vintage being left for thee?
No: she's an infamous, lewd prostitute:
I loath her at my soul.

GONSALVO - I can forbear
No longer: swallow down thy lie, foul villain.

[They fight off the stage. Exeunt.

JULIA - Help, help!

AMIDEO - Here is that witch, whose fatal beauty
Began the mischief; she shall pay for all.

[Goes to kill JULIA.

HIPPOLITO - I hate her for it more than thou canst do;
But cannot see her die, my master loves.

[Goes between with her sword.

Enter GONSALVO, following Don RODORICK, who falls.

Don RODORICK - So, now I am at rest:—
I feel death rising higher still, and higher,
Within my bosom; every breath I fetch
Shuts up my life within a shorter compass,
And, like the vanishing sound of bells, grows less
And less each pulse, 'till it be lost in air.

[Swoons away.

GONSALVO - Down at your feet, much injured innocence,
I lay that sword, which—

JULIA - Take it up again;
It has not done its work 'till I am killed:
For ever, ever, thou hast robbed me of
That man, that only man, whom I could love:
Dost thou thus court thy mistress? thus oblige her?
All thy obligements have been fatal yet,
Yet the most fatal now would most oblige me.
Kill me:—yet I am killed before in him.
I lie there on the ground; cold, cold, and pale:
That death, I die in Roderick, is far
More pleasant than that life, I live in Julia.
—See how he stands—when he is bid dispatch me!
How dull! how spiritless! that sloth possest
Thee not, when thou didst kill my Roderick.

GONSALVO - I'm too unlucky to converse with men:
I'll pack together all my mischiefs up,
Gather with care each little remnant of them,
That none of them be left behind: Thus loaded,
Fly to some desert, and there let them loose,
Where they may never prey upon mankind.
But you may make my journey shorter:—Take
This sword; 'twill shew you how:—

Jul:I'll gladly set you on your way:—
[Takes his sword.

Enter three of RODORICK'S servants.

1st SERVANT - Make haste; he's now unarmed, we may with ease
Revenge my master's death.

JULIA - Now these shall do it.

GONSALVO - I'll die by none but you.

HIPPOLITO - O here, take my sword, sir.

AMIDEO - He shall have mine.

[Both give their swords to GONSALVO.

Enter MANUEL.

MANUEL - Think not of death.
We'll live and conquer.

[They beat them off.

MANUEL - These fellows, though beat off, will strait return
With more; we must make haste to save ourselves.

HIPPOLITO - 'Tis far to the town,
And, ere you reach it, you will be discovered.

GONSALVO - My life's a burden to me, were not Julia's
Concerned; but, as it is, she, being present,
Will be found accessary to his death.

MANUEL - See where a vessel lies, not far from shore;
And near at hand a boat belonging to her;
Let's haste aboard, and what with prayers and gifts
Buy our concealment there:—Come, Julia.

GONSALVO - Alas, she swoons away upon the body.

MANUEL - The night grows on apace; we'll take her in
Our arms, and bear her hence.

[Exeunt GONSALVO, and the boys, with MANUEL, carrying JULIA.

The Servants enter again.

1st SERVANT - They are all gone, we may return with safety:
Help me to bear the body to the town.

2nd SERVANT - He stirs, and breathes a little; there may be
Some hope.

3rd SERVANT - The town's far off, and the evening cold.
Let's carry him to the ship.

1st SERVANT - Haste then away:
Things, once resolved, are ruined by delay.

[Exeunt.

SCENE I - The Scene Lying in a Carrack

Enter a Pirate and the Captain.

PIRATE - Welcome a ship-board, captain; you staid long.

CAPTAIN - No longer than was necessary for shifting trades;
To change me from a robber to a pirate.

PIRATE - There's a fair change wrought in you since yesterday morning;
Then you talked of nothing but repentance, and amendment of life.

CAPTAIN - 'Faith, I have considered better on't: for,
Conversing a whole day together with honest men,
I found them all so poor and beggarly,
That a civil person would be ashamed to be seen with them:—
But you come from Don Roderick's cabin; what hopes have you of his life?

PIRATE - No danger of it, only loss of blood had made him faint away; he called for you.

CAPTAIN - Well, are his jewels and his plate brought in?

PIRATE - They are. When hoist we sails?

CAPTAIN - At the first break of day:
When we are got out clear, we'll seize on Roderick and his men:
They are not many, but fear may make them desperate.

PIRATE - We may take them, when they are laid to sleep.

CAPTAIN - 'Tis well advised.

PIRATE - I forgot to tell you, sir,
That a little before Don Roderick was brought in,
A company of gentlemen (pursued it seems by justice)
Procured our boat to row them hither.
Two of them carried a very fair lady betwixt them,
Who was either dead, or swooned.

CAPTAIN - We'll sell them altogether to the Turk,—at least I'll tell them so. [Aside.

PIRATE - Pray, sir, let us reserve the lady to our own uses;
It were a shame to good catholicks to give her up to infidels.

CAPTAIN - Don Roderick's door opens; I'll speak to him.

The Scene draws, and discovers the Captains cabin;

RODORICK on a bed, and two Servants by him.

CAPTAIN - How is it with the brave Don Roderick? Do you want anything?

Don RODORICK - I have too much Of that I would not, love;
And what I would have, that I want, revenge. I must be set ashore.

CAPTAIN - That you may, sir; But our own safety must be thought on first.

[One enters, and whispers the Captain.

CAPTAIN - I come:—Seignior, think you are lord here, and command all freely.

[Exeunt Captain and Pirates.

Don RODORICK - He does well to bid me think so: I am of opinion
We are fallen into huckster's hands.

1st SERVANT - Indeed he talked suspiciously enough; He half denied to land us.

Don RODORICK - These, Pedro, are your confiding men—

2nd SERVANT - I think them still so.

Don RODORICK - Would I were from them.

2nd SERVANT - 'Tis impossible To attempt it now; you have not strength enough To walk.

Don RODORICK - That venture must be mine: We're lost, If we stay here to-morrow.

2nd SERVANT - I hope better.

1st SERVANT - One whom I saw among 'em, to my knowledge, Is a notorious robber.

2nd SERVANT - He looked so like a gentleman, I could not know him then.

Don RODORICK - What became of Julia when I fell?

1st SERVANT - We left her weeping over you, till we Were beaten off; but she, and those with her,
Were gone when we returned.

Don RODORICK - Too late I find,
I wronged her in my thoughts. I'm every way
A wretched man:—
Something we must resolve on, ere we sleep;
Draw in the bed, I feel the cold.

[Bed drawn in.

Exeunt.

SCENE II

Enter GONSALVO, MANUEL, HIPPOLITO and AMIDEO.

HIPPOLITO - Nay, 'tis too true; for, peeping through a chink,
I saw Don Roderick lying on a bed,
Not dead, as we supposed, but only hurt;
So waited on as spoke him master here.

MANUEL - Was there ever so fatal an adventure!
To fly into that very ship, for refuge,
Where the only person, we would shun, commands!
This mischief is so strange, it could not happen,
But was the plot and juggle of our fate,
To free itself, and cast the blame on us.

GONSALVO - This is not yet our fortune's utmost malice;
The gall remains behind. This ship was that,
Which yesterday was mine; I can see nothing
Round me, but what's familiar to my eyes;
Only the persons new: Which makes me think,
Twas seized upon by Roderick, to revenge
Himself on me.

MANUEL - Tis wonderful indeed.

AMIDEO - The only comfort is, we are not known;
For when we entered it was dark.

HIPPOLITO - That comfort
Is of as short continuance as the night;
The day will soon discover us.

MANUEL - Some way must be invented to get out.

HIPPOLITO - Fair Julia, sadly pining by herself.
Sits on her bed; tears falling from her eyes,
As silently as dews in dead of night.
All we consult of must be kept from her:
That moment, that she knows of Roderick's life,
Dooms us to certain death.

MANUEL - 'Tis well considered.

GONSALVO - For my part, were not you and she concerned,
I look upon my life, like an estate,
So charged with debts, it is not worth the keeping.

We cannot long be undiscovered by them;
Let us then rush upon them on the sudden,
(All hope of safety placed in our despair)
And gain quick victory, or speedy death.

MANUEL - Consider first, the impossibility
Of the attempt; four men, and two poor boys,
(Which, added to our number, make us weaker)
Against ten villains, more resolved for death,
Than any ten among our holiest priests.
Stay but a little longer, till they all
Disperse to rest within their several cabins;
Then more securely we may set upon them,
And kill them half, before the rest can wake:
By this means too, the boys are useful for us,
For they can cut the throats of sleeping men.

HIPPOLITO - Now have I the greatest temptation in the world to reveal,
Thou art a woman. [To AMIDEO.

AMIDEO - If 'twere not for thy beauty, my master should know,
What a man he keeps. [To HIPPOLITO.

HIPPOLITO - Why should we have recourse to desperate ways,
When safer may be thought on?
'Tis like giving the extreme unction.
In the beginning of a sickness;
Can you imagine to find all asleep?
The wicked joy, of having such a booty
In their possession, will keep some awake;
And some, no doubt, will watch with wounded
Roderick.

AMIDEO - What would your wisdom now propose?

HIPPOLITO - To say
That some of us are sea-sick; (your complexion
Will make the excuse for us who are less fair:)
So, by good words and promises, procure
We may be set ashore, ere morning come.

AMIDEO - O, the deep reasons of the grave Hippolito!—
As if 'twere likely, in so calm a season,
We should be sick so soon; or, if we were,
Whom should we chuse among us to go tell it?
For whoe'er ventures out must needs be known:
Or, if none knew us, can you think that pirates
Will let us go upon such easy terms,
As promising rewards?—Let me advise you.

HIPPOLITO - Now, we expect an oracle.

AMIDEO - Here are bundles,
Of canvas and of cloth, you see lie by us;
In which one of us shall sew up the rest,
Only some breathing place, for air, and food:
Then call the pirates in, and tell them, we,
For fear, had drowned ourselves: And when we come
To the next port, find means to bring us out.

HIPPOLITO - Pithily spoken!
As if you were to bind up marble statues,
Which only bore the shapes of men without,
And had no need of ever easing nature.

GONSALVO - There's but one way left, that's this;—
You know the rope, by which the cock-boat's tied,
Goes down by the stern, and now, we are at anchor,
There sits no pilot to discover us;
My counsel is, to go down by the ladder,
And, being once there, unloose, and row to shore.

MANUEL - This, without doubt, were best; but there lies ever
Some one, or more, within the boat, to watch it.

GONSALVO - I'll slide down first, and run the venture of it;
You shall come after me, if there be need,
To give me succour.

MANUEL - 'Tis the only way.

GONSALVO - Go in to Julia, then, and first prepare her,
With knowledge of the pirates, and the danger
Her honour's in, among such barbarous people.

MANUEL - Leave it to me.

AMIDEO - Hippolito and Julia,
My rivals, like two pointed rocks appear;
And I, through both, must to Gonsalvo steer. [Aside.

[Exeunt all but HIPPOLITA.

HIPPOLITO - As from some steep and dreadful precipice
The frighted traveller casts down his eyes,
And sees the ocean at so great a distance,
It looks as if the skies were sunk below him;
Yet if some neighbouring shrub (how weak soe'er)
Peeps up, his willing eyes stop gladly there,
And seem to ease themselves, and rest upon it:
So, in my desperate state, each little comfort
Preserves me from despair. Gonsalvo strove not

With greater care to give away his Julia,
Than I have done to part with my Gonsalvo;
Yet neither brought to pass our hateful wish.
Then, we may meet, since different ways we move,
Chasing each other in the maze of love.

[Exit.

SCENE III

Enter Don RODORICK, carried by two Servants.

1st SERVANT - It was the only way that could be thought on,
To get down by the ladder to the boat.

2nd SERVANT - You may thank me for that invention.

Don RODORICK - What a noise is here, when the least breath's
As dangerous as a tempest.

2nd SERVANT - If any of those rogues should hear him talk,
In what a case were we?

Don RODORICK - O, patience! patience!—This ass brays out for silence.

Enter, at the other end, MANUEL, leading JULIA, GONSALVO, HIPPOLITO, and AMIDEO.

GONSALVO - Hark! what noise is that? go softly.

[They meet on the middle of the stage.

Don RODORICK - Who's here? I am betrayed! and nothing grieves me,
But I want strength to die with honour.

JULIA - Roderick!
Is it thy voice, my love?—Speak, and resolve me,
Whether thou livest, or I am dead with thee?

MANUEL - Kill him, and force our way.

Don RODORICK - Is Manuel there?
Hold up my arm, that I may make one thrust
At him, before I die.

GONSALVO - Since we must fall,
We'll sell our lives as dearly as we can.

1st SERVANT - And we'll defend our master to the last.
[Fight.

Enter Pirates, without their Captain.

1st PIRATE - What's the meaning of this uproar? Quarrelling
Amongst yourselves at midnight?

2nd PIRATE - We are come in a fit time to decide the difference.

MANUEL - Hold, gentlemen! we're equally concerned.
[To RODORICK'S Servants.
We for our own, you for your master's safety;
If we join forces, we may then resist them,
If not, both sides are ruined.

1st SERVANT - We agree.

GONSALVO - Come o'er on our side then. [They join.

1st PIRATE - A mischief on our captain's drowsiness;
We're lost, for want of him! [They fight.

GONSALVO - Dear madam, get behind; while you are safe,
We cannot be o'ercome. [To JULIA.

[They drive off the Pirates, and follow them off.
RODORICK remains on the ground.

Don RODORICK - I had much rather my own life were lost,
Than Manuel's were preserved.

Enter the Pirates, retreating before GONSALVO, &c.

1ST PIRATE - All's lost! they fight like devils, and our captain
Yet sleeping in his bed.

2ND PIRATE - Here lies Don Roderick;
If we must die, we'll not leave him behind.

[Goes to kill him.

JULIA - O, spare my Roderick's life; and, in exchange,
Take mine! I put myself within your power,
To save or kill.

1ST PIRATE - So, here's another pawn,
For all our safeties.

MANUEL - Heaven! what has she done?

GONSALVO - Let go the lady, or expect no mercy!—The least drop of her blood is worth all yours.
And mine together.

1ST PIRATE - I am glad you think so:—
Either deliver up your sword, or mine
Shall pierce her heart this moment.

GONSALVO - Here, here, take it.

MANUEL - You are not mad, to give away all hopes

[MANUEL holds him

Of safety and defence, from us, from her, and from yourself, at once!

GONSALVO - When she is dead,
What is there worth defending?

MANUEL - Will you trust
A pirate's promise, sooner than your valour?

GONSALVO - Anything, rather than see her in danger.

1ST PIRATE- Nay, if you dispute the matter!—

[Holds his sword to her breast.

GONSALVO - I yield, I yield!—Reason to love must bow:
Love, that gives courage, can make cowards too!

[Gives his sword.

JULIA - O, strange effect of a most generous passion!

Don RODORICK - His enemies themselves must needs admire it.

MANUEL - Nay, if Gonsalvo makes a fashion of it,
'Twill be valour to die tamely. [Gives his.

HIPPOLITO - I am for dying too with my dear master.

AMIDEO - My life will go as easily as a fly's;
The least fillip does it in this fright.

1ST PIRATE - One call our captain up: Tell him, he
deserves little of the booty.

JULIA - It has so much prevailed upon my soul,
I ever must acknowledge it. [To GONSALVO.

Don RODORICK - Julia has reason, if she love him; yet, I find I cannot bear it. [Aside.

GONSALVO - Say but, you love me; I am more than paid.

JULIA - You ask that only thing, I cannot give;—
Were I not Roderick's first, I should be yours;
My violent love for him, I know, is faulty;
Yet passion never can be placed so ill,
But that to change it is the greater crime.
Inconstancy is such a guilt, as makes
That very love suspected, which it brings;
It brings a gift, but 'tis of ill-got wealth,
The spoils of some forsaken lover's heart.
Love, altered once, like blood let out before,
Will lose its virtue, and can cure no more.

GONSALVO - In those few minutes which I have to live,
To be called yours, is all I can enjoy.
Roderick receives no prejudice by that;
I would but make some small acquaintance here,
For fear I never should enquire you out
In that new world, which we are going to.

AMIDEO - Then, I can hold no longer;—You desire,
In death, to be called hers; and all I wish,
Is, dying, to be yours.

HIPPOLITO - You'll not discover? [Aside.

AMIDEO - See here the most unfortunate of women,
That Angelina, whom you all thought lost;
And lost she was indeed, when she beheld
Gonsalvo first.

ALL - How? Angelina!

Don RODORICK - Ha! My sister!

AMIDEO - I thought to have fled love in flying Manuel,
But love pursued me in Gonsalvo's shape:
For him, I ventured all that maids hold dear;
The opinion of my modesty, and virtue,
My loss of fortune, and my brother's love.
For him, I have exposed myself to dangers,
Which, great themselves, yet greater would appear,
If you could see them through a woman's fear.
But why do I my right by dangers prove?
The greatest argument for love is love:
That passion, Julia, while he lives, denies,
He should refuse to give her when he dies:
Yet grant he did his life to her bequeath,
May I not claim my share of him in death?
I only beg, when all the glory's gone,
The heatless beams of a departing sun.

GONSALVO - Never was passion, hid so modestly,
So generously revealed.

MANUEL - We're now a chain of lovers linked in death;
Julia goes first, Gonsalvo hangs on her,
And Angelina holds upon Gonsalvo,
As I on Angelina.

HIPPOLITO - Nay, here's Honoria too:—You look on me with wonder in your eyes,
To see me here, and in this strange disguise.

JULIA - What new miracle is this? Honoria!

MANUEL - I left you with my aunt at Barcelona,
And thought, ere this, you had been married to
The rich old man, Don Estevan de Gama.

HIPPOLITO - I ever had a strange aversion for him:
But when Gonsalvo landed there, and made
A kind of courtship, (though, it seems, in jest,)
It served to conquer me; which Estevan
Perceiving, pressed my aunt to haste the marriage.
What should I do? My aunt importuned me
For the next day: Gonsalvo, though I loved him,
Knew not my love; nor was I sure his courtship
Was not the effect of a bare gallantry.

GONSALVO - Alas! how grieved I am, that slight address
Should make so deep impression on your mind,
In three days time!

HIPPOLITO - That accident, in which
You saved my life, when first you saw me, caused it,
Though now the story be too long to tell.
Howe'er it was, hearing that night, you lay
Aboard your ship, thus, as you see, disguised,
In clothes belonging to my youngest nephew,
I rose ere day, resolved to find you out,
And, if I could, procure to wait on you
Without discovery of myself: but fortune
Crossed all my hopes.

GONSALVO - It was that dismal night
Which tore my anchor up, and tossed my ship,
Past hope of safety, many days together,
Until at length it threw me on this port.

HIPPOLITO - I will not tell you what my sorrows were,
To find you gone; but there was now no help.
Go back again, I durst not; but, in fine,

Thought best, as fast as my weak legs would bear me,
To come to Alicant, and find my sister,
Unknown to any else: But, being near
The city, I was seized upon by thieves,
From whom you rescued me. The rest you know.

GONSALVO - I know too much indeed for my repose.

Enter Captain.

CAPTAIN - Do you know me?

GONSALVO - Now I look better on thee,
Thou seemest a greater villain than I thought thee.

JULIA - 'Tis he!

HIPPOLITO - That bloody wretch, that robbed us in
The woods.

GONSALVO - Slave! darest thou lift thy hand against me?
Darest thou touch any one whom he protects,
Who gave thee life? But I accuse myself,
Not thee: The death of all these guiltless persons
Became my crime, that minute when I spared thee.

CAPTAIN - It is not all your threats can alter me
From what I have resolved.

GONSALVO - Begin, then, first with me.

CAPTAIN - I will, by laying here my sword.
[Lays his sword at Gonsalvo's feet.

All: What means this sudden change?

CAPTAIN - Tis neither new, nor sudden. From that time
You gave me life, I watched how to repay it;
And Roderick's servant gave me speedy means
To effect my wish: For, telling me, his master
Meant a revenge on you, and on Don Manuel,
And then to seize on Julia, and depart,
I proffered him my aid to seize a vessel;
And having, by enquiry, found out yours,
Acquainted first the captain with my purpose,
To make a seeming mastery of the ship.

MANUEL - How durst he take your word?

CAPTAIN - That I secured,
By letting him give notice to the ships

That lay about: This done, knowing the place
You were to fight on was behind the rock,
Not far from thence, I, and some chosen men,
Lay out of sight, that, if foul play were offered,
We might prevent it:
But came not in; because, when there was need,
Don Manuel, who was nearer, stepped before me.

GONSALVO - Then the boat, which seemed
To lie by chance, hulling not far from shore,
Was placed by your direction there?

CAPTAIN - It was.

GONSALVO - You're truly noble; and I owe much more
Than my own life and fortunes to your worth.

CAPTAIN - 'Tis time I should restore their liberty
To such of yours, as yet are seeming prisoners.
I'll wait on you again. [Exit Captain.

Don RODORICK - My enemies are happy; and the storm,
Prepared for them, must break upon my head.

GONSALVO - So far am I from happiness, heaven knows
My griefs are doubled!
I stand engaged in hopeless love to Julia;
In gratitude to these:—
Here I have given my heart, and here I owe it.

HIPPOLITO - Dear master, trouble not yourself for me;
I ever made your happiness my own;
Let Julia witness with what faith I served you.
When you employed me in your love to her,
I gave your noble heart away, as if
It had been some light gallant's, little worth:
Not that I loved you less than Angelina,
But myself less than you.

GONSALVO - Wonder of honour!
Of which my own was but a fainter shadow.
When I gave Julia, whom I could not keep,
You fed a fire within, with too rich fuel,
In giving it your heart to prey upon;
The sweetest offering that was ever burnt
Since last the Phoenix died.

HIPPOLITO - If Angelina knew, like me, the pride
Of noble minds, which is to give, not take,
Like me she would be satisfied, her heart
Was well bestowed, and ask for no return.

AMIDEO - Pray, let my heart alone; you'll use it as
The gipsies do our money;
If they once touch it, they have power upon't.

Enter the Servant, who appeared in the first act with GONSALVO.

SERVANT - O, my dear lord, Gonsalvo de Peralta!

Don RODORICK - De Peralta, said you? You amaze me!

GONSALVO - Why? Do you know that family in Seville?

Don RODORICK - I am myself the elder brother of it.

GONSALVO - Don Rodorick de Peralta!

Don RODORICK - I was so,
Until my mother died, whose name, de Sylva,
I chose, (our custom not forbidding it)
Three years ago, when I returned from Flanders:
I came here to possess a fair estate,
Left by an aunt, her sister; for whose sake
I take that name; and liked the place so well,
That never since have I returned to Seville.

GONSALVO - 'Twas then that change of name, which caused my letters
All to miscarry. What an happy tempest
Was this, which would not let me rest at Seville,
But blew me farther on, to see you here!

AMIDEO - Brother, I come to claim a sister's share:
but you're too near me, to be nearer now.

GONSALVO - In my room, let me beg you to receive Don Manuel.

AMIDEO - I take it half unkindly,
You give me from yourself so soon: Don Manuel,
I know, is worthy, and, but yesterday,
Preserved my life; but, it will take some time
To change my heart.

MANUEL - I'll watch it patiently, as chemists do
Their golden birth; and, when 'tis changed, receive it
With greater care than they their rich elixir,
Just passing from one vial to another.

Don RODORICK - Julia is still my brother's, though I lose her.

GONSALVO - You shall not lose her; Julia was born
For none but you;

And I for none but my Honoria:
Julia is yours by inclination;
And I, by conquest, am Honoria's.

HONORIA - 'Tis the most glorious one that e'er was made:
And I no longer will dispute my happiness.

Don RODORICK - Julia, you know my peevish jealousies;
I cannot promise you a better husband
Than you have had a servant.

JULIA - I receive you with all your faults.

Don RODORICK - And think, when I am froward,
My sullen humour punishes itself:
I'm like a day in March, sometimes o'ercast
With storms, but then the after clearness is
The greater. The worst is, where I love most,
The tempest falls most heavy.

JULIA - Ah! what a little time to love is lent! Yet half that time is in unkindness spent.

Don RODORICK - That you may see some hope of my amendment,
I give my friendship to Don Manuel, ere
My brother asks, or he himself desires it.

MANUEL - I'll ever cherish it.

GONSALVO - Since, for my sake, you become friends, my care
Shall be to keep you so. You, captain, shall
Command this carrack, and, with her, my fortunes.
You, my Honoria, though you have an heart
Which Julia left, yet think it not the worse;
'Tis not worn out, but polished by the wearing.
Your merit shall her beauty's power remove;
Beauty but gains, obligement keeps our love.

[Exeunt.

John Dryden – A Short Biography

John Dryden was born on August 9th, 1631 in the village rectory of Aldwincle near Thrapston in
Northamptonshire, where his maternal grandfather was Rector of All Saints Church.

Dryden was the eldest of fourteen children born to Erasmus Dryden and wife Mary Pickering,
paternal grandson of Sir Erasmus Dryden, 1st Baronet (1553–1632) and wife Frances Wilkes, Puritan
landowning gentry who supported the Puritan cause and Parliament.

As a boy Dryden lived in the nearby village of Titchmarsh, Northamptonshire where it is probable
that he received his first education.

In 1644 he was sent to Westminster School as a King's Scholar where his headmaster was Dr. Richard Busby, a charismatic teacher but severe disciplinarian. Having recently been re-founded by Elizabeth I, Westminster now embraced a very different religious and political spirit encouraging royalism and high Anglicanism but as a humanist public school, it maintained a curriculum which trained pupils in the art of rhetoric and the presentation of arguments for both sides of a given issue. This skill would remain with Dryden and influence his later writing and thinking, as much of it displays these dialectical patterns.

His first published poem, whilst still at Westminster, was an elegy with a strong royalist flavour on the death of his schoolmate Henry, Lord Hastings from smallpox, and alludes to the execution of King Charles I, which took place on January 30th, 1649.

In 1650 Dryden was ready for University and travelled to Trinity College, Cambridge. Dryden's undergraduate years would almost certainly have followed the standard curriculum of classics, rhetoric, and mathematics.

Dryden obtained his BA in 1654, graduating top of the list for Trinity that year.

However family tragedy struck in June of the same year when Dryden's father died, leaving him some land which generated a small income, but not enough to live on.

Returning to London during The Protectorate, Dryden now obtained work with Cromwell's Secretary of State, John Thurloe. This may have been the result of influence exercised on his behalf by his cousin the Lord Chamberlain, Sir Gilbert Pickering.

At Cromwell's funeral on 23 November 1658 Dryden was in the company of the Puritan poets John Milton and Andrew Marvell. The setting was to be a sea change in English history. From Republic to Monarchy and from one set of lauded poets to what would soon become the Age of Dryden.

The start began later that year when Dryden published the first of his great poems, Heroic Stanzas (1658), a eulogy on Cromwell's death which is necessarily cautious and prudent in its emotional display.

With the Restoration of the Monarchy in 1660 Dryden celebrated in verse with Astraea Redux, an authentic royalist panegyric. In this work the interregnum is illustrated as a time of anarchy, and Charles is seen as the restorer of peace and order.

With the king now established Dryden moved quickly to place himself as the leading poet and critic of his day and transferred his allegiances to the new government.

Along with Astraea Redux, Dryden welcomed the new regime with two more panegyrics: To His Sacred Majesty: A Panegyric on his Coronation (1662) and To My Lord Chancellor (1662).

These panegyrics are occasional and written to celebrate events. Thus they are written for the nation rather than the self, but these and others put him in good standing for his eventual appointment as Poet Laureate, where a number of event poems would be required each year and speaking for the Nation and to the Nation would be the first order of duty.

These poems suggest that Dryden was looking to court a possible patron which would have given him an income and time to explore his creative ideas but no, his path instead would be to make a living in writing for publishers, not for the aristocracy, and thus ultimately for the reading public.

In November 1662 Dryden was proposed for membership in the Royal Society, and he was elected an early fellow. However, his inactivity and non payment of dues led to his expulsion in 1666.

On December 1st, 1663 Dryden married the Royalist sister of Sir Robert Howard—Lady Elizabeth Howard (died 1714). The marriage was at St. Swithin's, London, and the consent of the parents is noted on the license, though Lady Elizabeth was then about twenty-five. She was the object of some scandals, well or ill founded; it was said that Dryden had been bullied into the marriage by her brothers. A small estate in Wiltshire was settled upon them by her father. The lady's intellect and temper were apparently not good; her husband was treated as an inferior by those of her social status.

Dryden's works occasionally contain outbursts against the married state but also celebrations of the same. Little else is known of the intimate side of his marriage.

Both Dryden and his wife were warmly attached to their children. They had three sons: Charles (1666–1704), John (1668–1701), and Erasmus Henry (1669–1710). Lady Elizabeth Dryden survived her husband, but went insane soon after his death and died in 1714.

With the re-opening of the theatres after the Puritan ban, Dryden began to also write plays. His first play, The Wild Gallant, appeared in 1663 but was not successful. From 1668 on he was contracted to produce three plays a year for the King's Company, in which he became a shareholder. During the 1660s and '70s, theatrical writing was his main source of income. He led the way in Restoration comedy, his best-known works being Marriage à la Mode (1672), as well as heroic tragedy and regular tragedy, in which his greatest success was All for Love (1678). Dryden was never fully satisfied with his theatrical writings and frequently suggested that his talents were wasted on unworthy audiences.

Certainly therefore fame as a poet looked more rewarding. In 1667, around the same time his dramatic career began, he published Annus Mirabilis, a lengthy historical poem which described the English defeat of the Dutch naval fleet and the Great Fire of London in 1666. It was a modern epic in pentameter quatrains that established him as the pre-eminent poet of his generation, and was crucial in his attaining the posts of Poet Laureate (1668) and then historiographer royal (1670).

When the Great Plague of London closed the theatres in 1665 Dryden retreated to Wiltshire where he wrote Of Dramatick Poesie (1668), arguably the best of his unsystematic prefaces and essays. Dryden constantly defended his own literary practice, and Of Dramatick Poesie, the longest of his critical works, takes the form of a dialogue in which four characters–each based on a prominent contemporary, with Dryden himself as 'Neander'—debate the merits of classical, French and English drama.

He felt strongly about the relation of the poet to tradition and the creative process, and his heroic play Aureng-zebe (1675) has a prologue which denounces the use of rhyme in serious drama. His play All for Love (1678) was written in blank verse, and was to immediately follow Aureng-Zebe.

On December 18th, 1679 he was attacked in Rose Alley near his home in Covent Garden by thugs hired by fellow poet, John Wilmot, 2nd Earl of Rochester, with whom he had a long-standing conflict.

Wilmot was constantly in and out of favour with the King and his own poetry was often bawdy, lewd, even obscene and made fun of the King who would often exile him from Court.

Dryden's greatest achievements were in satiric verse: the mock-heroic Mac Flecknoe, a more personal product of his Laureate years, was a lampoon circulated in manuscript and an attack on the playwright Thomas Shadwell. Dryden's main goal in the work is to "satirize Shadwell, ostensibly for his offenses against literature but more immediately we may suppose for his habitual badgering of him on the stage and in print." It is not a belittling form of satire, but rather one which makes his object great in ways which are unexpected, transferring the ridiculous into poetry. This line of satire continued with Absalom and Achitophel (1681) and The Medal (1682). Other major works from this period are the religious poems Religio Laici (1682), written from the position of a member of the Church of England; his 1683 edition of Plutarch's Lives, translated From the Greek by Several Hands in which he introduced the word biography to English readers; and The Hind and the Panther, (1687) which celebrates his conversion to Roman Catholicism.

He wrote Britannia Rediviva celebrating the birth of a son and heir to the Catholic King and Queen on June 10th, 1688. When later in the same year James II was deposed in the Glorious Revolution, Dryden's refusal to take the oaths of allegiance to the new monarchs, William and Mary, which left him out of favour at court and he had to leave his post as Poet Laureate. Thomas Shadwell, his despised rival, succeeded him. Dryden, England's greatest literary figure, was now forced to give up his public offices and live by the proceeds of his pen alone.

Dryden was an excellent translator with his own style which brought the ire of many critics. Many felt he would embellish or expand anything he felt short or curt. Dryden did not feel such expansion was a fault, arguing that as Latin is a naturally concise language it cannot be duly represented by a comparable number of words in the much larger English vocabulary. He continued with his task of translating works by Horace, Juvenal, Ovid, Lucretius, and Theocritus, a task which he found far more satisfying than writing for the stage.

In 1694 he began work on what would be his most ambitious and defining work as translator, The Works of Virgil (1697), which was published by subscription. The publication of the translation of Virgil was a national event and brought Dryden the sum of £1,400.

His final translations appeared in the volume Fables Ancient and Modern (1700), a series of episodes from Homer, Ovid, and Boccaccio, as well as modernised adaptations from Geoffrey Chaucer interspersed with Dryden's own poems. As a translator, he made great literary works in the older languages available to readers of English.

John Dryden died on May 12th, 1700, and was initially buried in St. Anne's cemetery in Soho, before being exhumed and reburied in Westminster Abbey ten days later. He was the subject of poetic eulogies, such as Luctus Brittannici: or the Tears of the British Muses; for the Death of John Dryden, Esq. (London, 1700), and The Nine Muses.

He is seen as dominating the literary life of Restoration England to such a point that the period came to be known in literary circles as the Age of Dryden. Walter Scott called him "Glorious John."

Dryden was the dominant literary figure and influence of his age. He established the heroic couplet as a standard form of English poetry by writing successful satires, religious pieces, fables, epigrams, compliments, prologues, and plays with it; he also introduced the alexandrine and triplet into the form. In his poems, translations, and criticism, he established a poetic diction appropriate to the heroic couplet—Auden referred to him as "the master of the middle style"—that was a model for his contemporaries and for much of the 18th century. The considerable loss felt by the English literary community at his death was evident in the elegies written about him. Dryden's heroic couplet went on to become the dominant poetic form of the 18th century.

What Dryden achieved in his poetry was neither the emotional excitement of the early nineteenth-century romantics nor the intellectual complexities of the metaphysicals. Although he uses formal structures such as heroic couplets, he tried to recreate the natural rhythm of speech, and he knew that different subjects need different kinds of verse. In his preface to Religio Laici he says that "the expressions of a poem designed purely for instruction ought to be plain and natural, yet majestic... The florid, elevated and figurative way is for the passions; for (these) are begotten in the soul by showing the objects out of their true proportion.... A man is to be cheated into passion, but to be reasoned into truth."

Perhaps the following illustrates Dryden and his life—"The way I have taken, is not so streight as Metaphrase, nor so loose as Paraphrase: Some things too I have omitted, and sometimes added of my own. Yet the omissions I hope, are but of Circumstances, and such as wou'd have no grace in English; and the Addition, I also hope, are easily deduc'd from Virgil's Sense. They will seem (at least I have the Vanity to think so), not struck into him, but growing out of him".

John Dryden – A Concise Bibliography

Astraea Redux, 1660
The Wild Gallant (comedy), 1663
The Indian Emperour (tragedy), 1665
Annus Mirabilis (poem), 1667
The Enchanted Island (comedy), 1667, with William D'Avenant from Shakespeare's The Tempest
Secret Love, or The Maiden Queen, 1667
An Essay of Dramatick Poesie, 1668
An Evening's Love (comedy), 1668
Tyrannick Love (tragedy), 1669
The Conquest of Granada, 1670
The Assignation, or Love in a Nunnery, 1672
Marriage à la mode, 1672
Amboyna, or the Cruelties of the Dutch to the English Merchants, 1673
The Mistaken Husband (comedy), 1674
Aureng-zebe, 1675
All for Love, 1678
Oedipus (heroic drama), 1679, an adaptation with Nathaniel Lee of Sophocles' Oedipus
Absalom and Achitophel, 1681
The Spanish Fryar, 1681
Mac Flecknoe, 1682
The Medal, 1682
Religio Laici, 1682
To the Memory of Mr. Oldham, 1684
Threnodia Augustalis, 1685
The Hind and the Panther, 1687
A Song for St. Cecilia's Day, 1687
Britannia Rediviva, 1688, written to mark the birth of a Prince of Wales.
Amphitryon, 1690

Don Sebastian (play), 1690
Creator Spirit, by whose aid, 1690. Translation of Rabanus Maurus' Veni Creator Spiritus
King Arthur, 1691
Cleomenes, 1692
The Art of Satire, 1693
Love Triumphant, 1694
The Works of Virgil, 1697
Alexander's Feast, 1697
Fables, Ancient and Modern, 1700

www.ingramcontent.com/pod-product-compliance
Lightning Source LLC
Chambersburg PA
CBHW060141050426
42448CB00010B/2245